Iranian Identity,
American Experience

PHILOSOPHY OF RACE

Series Editor: George Yancy, Emory University

Editorial Board: Sybol Anderson, Barbara Applebaum, Alison Bailey, Chike Jeffers, Janine Jones, David Kim, Emily S. Lee, Zeus Leonardo, Falguni A. Sheth, Grant Silva

The Philosophy of Race book series publishes interdisciplinary projects that center upon the concept of race, a concept that continues to have very profound contemporary implications. Philosophers and other scholars, more generally, are strongly encouraged to submit book projects that seriously address race and the process of racialization as a deeply embodied, existential, political, social, and historical phenomenon. The series is open to examine monographs, edited collections, and revised dissertations that critically engage the concept of race from multiple perspectives: sociopolitical, feminist, existential, phenomenological, theological, and historical.

Iranian Identity, American Experience: Philosophical Reflections on Race, Rights, Capabilities, and Oppression, by Roksana Alavi

The Weight of Whiteness: A Feminist Engagement with Privilege, Race, and Ignorance, by Alison Bailey

The Logic of Racial Practice: Explorations in the Habituation of Racism, edited by Brock Bahler

Hip-Hop as Philosophical Text and Testimony: Can I Get a Witness?, by Lissa Skitolsky

The Blackness of Black: Key Concepts in Critical Discourse, by William David Hart

Self-Definition: A Philosophical Inquiry from the Global South and Global North, by Teodros Kiros

A Phenomenological Hermeneutic of Antiblack Racism in The Autobiography of Malcolm X, by David Polizzi

Buddhism and Whiteness, edited by George Yancy and Emily McRae

Black Christology and the Quest for Authenticity: A Philosophical Appraisal, by John H. McClendon III

For Equals Only: Race, Equality, and the Equal Protection Clause, by Tina Fernandes Botts

Politics and Affect in Black Women's Fiction, by Kathy Glass

The Habits of Racism: A Phenomenology of Racism and Racialized Embodiment, by Helen Ngo

Philosophy and the Mixed Race Experience, edited by Tina Fernandes Botts D. Hill

The Post-Racial Limits of Memorialization: Toward a Political Sense of Mourning, by Alfred Frankowski

White Self-Criticality beyond Anti-racism: How Does It Feel to Be a White Problem?, edited by George Yancy

Iranian Identity, American Experience

Philosophical Reflections on Race, Rights, Capabilities, and Oppression

Roksana Alavi

LEXINGTON BOOKS
Lanham • Boulder • New York • London

Published by Lexington Books
An imprint of The Rowman & Littlefield Publishing Group, Inc.
4501 Forbes Boulevard, Suite 200, Lanham, Maryland 20706
www.rowman.com

6 Tinworth Street, London SE11 5AL, United Kingdom

Copyright © 2021 The Rowman & Littlefield Publishing Group, Inc.

All rights reserved. No part of this book may be reproduced in any form or by any electronic or mechanical means, including information storage and retrieval systems, without written permission from the publisher, except by a reviewer who may quote passages in a review.

British Library Cataloguing in Publication Information Available

Library of Congress Cataloging-in-Publication Data

Library of Congress Cataloging-in-Publication Data
Names: Alavi, Roksana, 1973- author.
Title: Iranian identity, American experience : philosophical reflections on race, rights, capabilities, and oppression / Roksana Alavi.
Description: Lanham, Maryland : Lexington Books, [2021] | Series: Philosophy of race | Includes bibliographical references and index. | Summary: "This multidisciplinary book brings the topics of rights, identity, and race together to examine what it means to be oppressed, how oppression works, and what we both as individuals and as a community can do about it, using the Iranian American community as a case study"— Provided by publisher.
Identifiers: LCCN 2020052734 (print) | LCCN 2020052735 (ebook) | ISBN 9781498575096 (cloth) | ISBN 9781498575102 (epub)
Subjects: LCSH: Iranians—United States. | Iranian Americans—Ethnic identity. | Iranian Americans—Social conditions.
Classification: LCC E184.I5 A43 2021 (print) | LCC E184.I5 (ebook) | DDC 305.891/55073—dc23
LC record available at https://lccn.loc.gov/2020052734
LC ebook record available at https://lccn.loc.gov/2020052735

To my daughter, Havah,
who was born when this project started.

Contents

Acknowledgments		ix
Introduction		xi
1	My Life in the Triangle	1
2	*What Are You?*: A Discussion on Race, Ethnicity, and (Iranian) Identity	22
3	Voluntary Oppression	53
4	Bridging the Gap Between Rights and Capabilities	74
5	Harms of Oppression	106
6	Responding to Oppression	119
Bibliography		129
Index		141
About the Author		151

Acknowledgments

As this book is being readied for press, we are fighting a global pandemic and racial injustice, and the United States presidential elections are less than a month away. Among so many hard losses this year, we also lost the great Supreme Court Justice Ruth Bader Ginsberg. Although many people have been moved to action, so many people are hurting. I am no different. Past traumas and the ongoing war on Black and Brown bodies, in addition to extra demands on me as both an academic and a single parent, made writing challenging during the pandemic. Through all of this, the series editor George Yancy never failed to email me with encouraging messages. Thank you, George.

Writing about oppression is difficult. Writing about oppression of one's own community and personal experiences is emotionally challenging. Perhaps that's another reason why this book has taken so long to get to this point. I want to take this time to acknowledge those who have helped me through this process in the last decade or so.

During the last couple of years as I especially focused on this book, my Dean, Martha Banz, at the University of Oklahoma College of Professional and Continuing Studies provided me with any assistance that she possibly could give me so I could have space to think and write. I also want to thank my friend, Karen Antell, who read and edited the earlier drafts, as well as the anonymous reviewer for their extensive and detailed comments.

Some portion of this work started in graduate school. I am grateful to my then advisor, Ann Cudd, and professors Thomas Tuozzo, Tony Genova, Rex Martin, and Mehrangiz Najafizadeh. Ann's help was and continues to be instrumental in my work, both personally and professionally.

There is also my family. I am grateful to my parents, Fred and Azar Alavi, for their support by being my co-parents, and their example of dedication and unconditional love. My partner, William J. Robb, who listened to my ideas, got me outside on hikes, and encouraged me on the days that the pandemic got the best of me. His patience, love and kindness are invaluable. Finally, my daughter Havah, who was born when this project was still an idea. Her unstoppable spirit pushes me forward.

Introduction

Since the 1979 Islamic revolution in Iran and the subsequent strained relations between the United States and Iran, Iranian American men have been stereotyped as being uncivilized, barbaric, untrustworthy, abusive, and aggressive, while Iranian American women have been stereotyped as being submissive victims who lack agency and need help. I was born in Iran but moved to the United States at age fifteen. Although I have lived in the United States for thirty years now and have not visited my home country even once, I still feel ashamed of telling people I am from Iran. And I am not alone. This common feeling of shame comes from the negative stereotypes against me and against those with whom I share a common identity. Like most communities of immigrants, we continually question our own identities, wondering what it means to belong to a nation or nations. Against this backdrop, I want to explore what it means to create an identity and, further, examine the significance of both personal and our social identities.

This book will cover many philosophical topics, including race, rights, capabilities, identity, and oppression and its harms. The philosophical literature is already replete with many works on all of these topics, but few have put rights, identity, and race together to provide a comprehensive view of what it means to be oppressed, how oppression works, and what we can do about it both as individuals and as a society. In this book, I will use my own community, Iranian Americans, as a case study to investigate what oppression means both politically and individually to determine how best to counteract it.

I will start by developing a theory of oppression that discusses oppression's inherent harms, a significant example being stereotyping, which is inflicted both externally and internally. I argue that those who are stereotyped, both negatively and positively, internalize social expectations and become what society expects of them. The internalization of inferiority leads to the attitudes, habits, and behaviors that the oppressor expects. Hence, the oppressed become their own oppressors, an experience common among many colonized peoples. When individuals internalize negative stereotypes about them, the harms of oppression continue long after the oppressor has ceased to actively perpetrate injustices.

Individuals' internalization of stereotypes stems from their sense of identity with a group that is stereotyped. The stereotypes about a particular group are closely related to the way the group is racially classified. I should note that stereotypes can also be positive but still morally problematic, and set up harmful expectations. I will discuss current theories of race to explain how even those who pass as a different race, such as Black people who pass as white or Iranian people who pass as Greek, are harmed by oppression due to the stereotypes against them.

In the scholarly studies of oppression today, we are often presented with a dichotomy between Blacks and white that ignores other people of color. Moreover, very little of the philosophical literature on race addresses the Iranian American population. This is confounded by the fact that the U.S. Census classification of Iranian Americans as white. We are told to choose "white" when filling out forms about our racial identity, but it is perfectly clear that we are not white in the United States. My appearance as not-white *others* me. My theory of oppression therefore addresses not only external oppression inflicted by institutions such as governments and the media, but also the everyday actions through which individuals engage in self-oppression.

In chapter 1, I discuss the nuances involved in being Iranian American in the United States and creating one's identity in the midst of overwhelmingly negative media portrayals of our community. In 1991, a decade after the Iran hostage crisis—and at the time that both American-born children of Iranian and non-Iranians, in America, were coming of age in the United States following the Islamic revolution in Iran—Hollywood gave us *Not Without My Daughter*, a film that shows Iranian men to be brutally abusive. More recently, the American entertainment industry has generated additional popular media views of Iran, Iranians, and Iranian Americans through the 2012 film *Argo* and the reality television show *Shahs of Sunset*, which debuted in 2012 on the *Bravo* network and is still continuing as of this writing in 2020. It is in the triangle between *Not Without My Daughter, Argo,* and *Shahs of Sunset* that I live and forge my identity. These stories create the boundaries that I must navigate every day. As Brown and Black people in America, we do not get individual stories. We get overgeneralized portrayals and stereotypical images. When a stabbing, shooting, or mass murder occurs, we immediately but secretly hope it was not perpetrated by one of our people. People of color in the United States know that we cannot truly be heard as individuals; every time we speak, we are assumed to be speaking for our entire race. The media tells one story about people of color. It is in this space that I internalize but also resist the negative stereotypes about me and my community.

In the United States, when you walk around with my particular shade of brown, you often hear the question *"what* are you?" Simply by being asked that question, I am dehumanized. I am turned into a "what"—a thing that needs to be identified, categorized, and placed in context. In chapter 2, I will explore the answer to this question, yet the question still bewilders me, and I still do not really know *what* I am. This bewilderment is prevalent among many people who share my shade of brown, especially those in the Middle Eastern community. As stated, we are all told to check the "white" box on forms that ask about our race, yet we do not experience the world as if we were white. Sally Haslanger's (2000) view resonates with me, because although she is not an eliminatavist about race, as Naomi Zack (2002) is, her view has elements of social interpretations. She argues that people do not *have* a race, but are *given* a race. One is racialized by one's bodily appearance and its perceived connection with a particular geographic area and, by virtue of this classification, one is harmed or benefited. I will argue for an *objectively constructed folk theory* of race, one that both accounts for one's position of harm or privilege in a racially hierarchical society and applies ordinary people's understanding of race.

In chapter 3, I will present a theory of oppression that closely parallels Ann Cudd's (1994, 2006) view, applying it to what Jean Harvey (1999) calls "civilized oppression." Cudd gives us four necessary and jointly sufficient criteria to help us recognize all kind of oppression. These criteria are harm, group membership, privilege group, and coercion. I propose four amendments to her view: (1) I replace coercion with a systematicity criterion. The systematicity criterion, according to Cudd, is implicit in her group membership criterion. (2) In addition to making the systematicity criterion explicit, I also remove the necessity of coercion as a criterion for all oppressive situations. (3) In Cudd's view, coercion is normative; in my view, harm is. (4) Harm is the violation of one's capabilities, which in my view are the bases for rights. The capabilities approach also gives a metaphysical background to Cudd's theory of oppression.

Chapter 4 introduces and develops the capabilities approach. I do two things in this chapter. First, I argue that capabilities generate rights. That is, if someone has the capability to do x, they should have the right to do x, as long as it does not violate the liberty principle. This understanding of rights and capabilities will give us a more comprehensive theory of justice and social analysis. I will also discuss several additional benefits of grounding rights in capabilities. Second, I will evaluate the situation of the Iranian American community via the capabilities approach and show how the harms of both microaggressions and cultural imperialism are not only substantial, but also have grave consequences on the lives of those who experience them. I will conclude the chapter by explaining how violations of individuals' capabilities, including through microaggressions, violate their rights.

Chapter 5 discusses the physical and emotional harms of oppression and shows that they can be either voluntarily or involuntarily inflicted. Although people who pass as white are not victims of direct harm, they internalize negative stereotypes and become their own oppressors. It is profoundly unsettling that a person who is not racialized as a member of a negatively stereotyped group is still deeply harmed by the negative stereotypes associated with them. For Iranian Americans, who live a double life of being *white* and *not-white*, the harms are often psychological and self-limiting rather than blatantly physical. Because stereotyping leads to self-shame and stereotype threat, even in the case of those who pass as white, a theory that does not include the coercion criterion explains oppression better than one that does. We inhibit our own capabilities without any force. To end racial oppression, then, we must not only address the political element of possessing rights, but also work at the individual level to bring everyone's capabilities to the threshold level of functioning.

In chapter 6, I will end the book with a discussion of forces that keep oppression in place and how to respond to them.

Chapter One

My Life in the Triangle

LIFE IN MY CORNER

Just about the time that I started really thinking about my lived experiences as a woman of color in the Midwest, Claudia Card visited the University of Oklahoma and presented her article on "Surviving Poverty," in which she describes her experiences growing up deeply impoverished in order to give a philosophical analysis of that experience (2014). Her phenomenological understanding of her own experience and its effect on developing a theoretical analysis of survival was quite moving. Soon thereafter, I became acquainted with George Yancy (2008) and his book *Black Bodies, White Gazes* (2008), in which he describes his lived experiences as a Black man embodying Blackness in the white world. Following in the footsteps of Card and Yancy, this book shares my lived experiences, explores their implications, and analyzes them using critical race theory. In addition, in her recent work, Naomi Zack (2017, 556) argues that one's personal narrative can be politically quite effective in ways that other political movements might not; "Narrative has the power to activate emotions, aspirations, and moral feelings that can motivate practical action." I hope that my narrative would do just that. I share Mariana Ortega's (2016) concern that I might be harshly criticized for this method of inquiry because it is not the norm in the discipline of philosophy, and I was not taught to "do" philosophy in this way. Philosophy is supposed to be objective, the so-called "view from nowhere" (as characterized by Nagel 1986), but it turns out that the "nowhere" simply describes the perspective of those who historically have been granted access to the world of academic philosophy: male and white. While maleness and whiteness of philosophy mask themselves as objective, the reality is that there isn't objectivity in this sense. The thick walls of objectivity do not allow the penetration of marginalized views, and ignores the particularities of experiences; the idea of objectivity in philosophy is very well protected.

Although I was taught that doing "real" philosophy means doing analytic philosophy, I believe there is room for other methodologies. With the phenomenological description I will provide, I aim to combine both analytical and phenomenological ways of doing philosophy. This disputed terrain is dangerous to navigate, but I am not sure how *not* to navigate this space. I know that both life and lived experiences have meanings; both affect the way we articulate our beliefs and thoughts and formulate our theoretical understanding. Just as science looks to data for theory, in philosophy, we too can use the information from our lived experiences for theory development. We each have access to unique information by virtue of our unique lived experiences.

If standpoint theory has taught us anything, it is that our social location gives us a view that is unique to our perspective. Standpoint theory gives us the kinds of knowledge that only some people in some corners of the world can access (Harding 1991, 2004, 2004a; Collins 2000). This does not mean that such knowledge is inaccessible to everyone else, but accessing it requires perspective-taking in very deep and intimate ways. Among standpoint theorists, according to Alison Wylie (2003, 28), there are two points of agreement:

> *First,* standpoint theory must not presuppose an *essentialist* definition of the social categories or collective in terms of which epistemically relevant standpoints are characterized.
>
> *Second,* it must not be aligned with a thesis of *automatic epistemic privilege*; standpoint theorists cannot claim that those who occupy particular standpoints (usually subdominant, oppressed, and marginalized standpoints) automatically know more, or know better, by virtue of their social, political location.

I agree that difference is not *necessarily* an epistemic privilege, nor does it give a particular knower a particular kind of power that others do not have. However, some perspectives see things that might not be easily visible to others. Our social placement does not necessarily give us epistemic privilege, but it may give us a perspective that allows us to perceive certain phenomena more easily. Perhaps standpoint theory adds to the methods of perception, and viewpoints, that we use to construct or gain knowledge. Wylie (2003, 33) reminds us of the feminist contribution to knowledge production, which illustrates the importance of standpoint theory:

> The recent history of feminist contributions to the social and life sciences illustrates how such a standpoint may fruitfully raise standards of empirical adequacy for hitherto unexamined presuppositions, expand the range of hypoth-

eses under consideration in ways that ultimately improve explanatory power, and open up new lines of inquiry.

It is to this aim that phenomenology can contribute to social and political evaluations and even broaden theory or develop new theories to explain events. In this chapter, I will describe my lived experiences and then, borrowing from the works of Latina and Black feminists, provide the implications of those lived experiences, including their effects on the process of my identity development.

My Life

My physical appearance as a Brown Iranian American woman in the United States at a predominantly white institution prompts others to ask questions, make assumptions, generate expectations, and resort to stereotypes about my background and history. As George Yancy (2008, 1) puts it, "I am contrary to the existential credo, an essence ('Blackness') that precedes my existence." In other words, contrary to the existential creed that states that each person creates their own meaning, path, identity, and agency, my appearance conjures for most people the stereotypical images they associated with bodies that look like mine. I, too, am judged as the "other" who does not belong to the "civilized" world, whose country of origin is unworthy of being treated as an equal member of the international community. In a private conversation President Trump even referred to many parts of the world as "shithole" countries, which is an indication of how he feels about people of color immigrating from non-white societies (Dawsey 2018). My ambiguously ethnic appearance brings with it the prescribed essence that's not mine—whether or not my ethnicity is "properly" categorized as Iranian American. The culture, religion, and even intelligence that others assign to me leave me little room to create my essence.

In a world created for whiteness, Brown bodies are seen as violent and lazy, and our minds as irrational and unintelligent. Brown bodies are to be feared, objectified, used, humiliated, and violated. People have seen the Brown bodies in the face of the Boston Marathon bomber, in the face of those who shamelessly behead innocent Americans and videotape it, in the face of wife beaters, drug dealers, and illegal immigrants. Looking *ambiguously Brown* means that "my body is confiscated within social spaces of meaning construction and social spaces of transversal interaction that are buttressed by a racist value-laden episteme. It is a peculiar experience to have one's body confiscated without physically being placed in chains" (Yancy 2008, 4). I have no control over how I am perceived. Having one's body interpreted is self-alienating. I have a choice of responses, but the most obvious ones form a double bind. If I point out instances of stereotype and overgeneralization, no matter how "nicely" I do so, the risk is very high that I will be reinterpreted with another stereotype: the angry, oversensitive Brown woman, which brings its own sense of shame at being *that person*. Yet if I say nothing, I fail to remedy my own self-alienation. These choices bring with them both the anxiety of how to overcome others' interpretation of one's being and the anger that accompanies a sense of hopelessness as one's identity is seized. These are examples of *racialized* trauma that "do not take the form of a racist spectacular event" where one can see horrible acts of atrocities being done against one's body (Yancy 2017, 587). So, whites fail to see them. However, they are no less traumatic than physical acts of violence that is experienced by the oppressed.

I am an Iranian-born naturalized U.S. citizen. I wish I could say that the only negative associations that others have regarding my identity are the 1979 Islamic revolution and the Iran hostage crisis. These events are foremost in many people's minds, and indeed, they continue to haunt me. Although the Iran hostage crisis happened four decades ago, its effects remain, and I deal with the ripples every time I introduce myself, walk into a new place, or post my profile picture in my online class.

In 1979, images of screaming, angry mobs of Iranians burning American flags while attacking the U.S. embassy bombarded television screens all over the world. For the next 444 days, more than sixty American diplomats and citizens were held hostage in Iran. They were finally freed on January 20, 1981. I was seven years old at the time and living in Iran. I do not recall the hostage crisis, but I do remember the unrest. My home country and my life changed more than any child or adult could imagine. Meanwhile, every day, news programs showed Americans the increasing number of days that their fellow citizens had been held hostage. Americans heard from President Carter who solicited the help of "other nations in condemning this act of violence, which is shocking and violates the moral and the legal standards of a civilized world" implying that Iran is not a civilized country and Iranians are not a civilized people (Carter 1980, para. 6). The actions of a small minority of extremists defined what Americans grew to think about Iranian people. Children who had not had the chance to learn anything else about Iran learned that whatever is connected with Iran is just bad news and were filled with fear and hatred. That was forty years ago, and the American perception of Iranians has not changed much since then.

Just a year after the hostage crisis, the war between Iran and Iraq started, lasting for eight years. My family immigrated to the United States in 1988, before the end of the war. I was fifteen years old and did not speak English. Relations between the United States and Iran were unfavorable, and Americans were not very fond of Iranians. In a poll conducted in 1989, "a decade after the Iranian revolution, the number of Americans who held an unfavorable opinion toward Iran had increased to 91 percent" (Mobasher 2012, 5). I now understand why my family instructed me to pass as Greek. Passing as another ethnicity had never even crossed my mind as a teenager coming to the "land of the free." There is a sense of irony that we went from pretending to support the Islamic revolution in Iran to avoid the wrath of morality police, to pretending to be Greek to avoid racism in the United States. The absurdity of living in that contradiction is dizzying and prompts an existential crisis of meaning. Even if only for a short time, a dreaded nihilism occupies the space where freedom and equality should be. Perhaps the Iranian and African American comedian Tehran's claim that "Persian is the new Black!" is not too far off (Soparvaz 2013).

Following the trauma of 9/11 and its aftermath, our community, and the individuals in it, have had to constantly recreate our identity and put our fragmented selves back together for the sake of our emotional and physical safety. Iranian American sociologist and anthropologist Mohsen Mobasher (2012, 3–4) writes:

> other than the relocation and internment of Japanese Americans after the attack on Pearl Harbor in 1941, and the post-9/11 treatment of Muslim Arabs from the Middle East, no other immigrant group in the most recent migration history of the United States from an "enemy state"—as proclaimed by the mainstream media, public opinion polls, and government officials—has been so politicized, publicly despised, stigmatized, and traumatized by the U.S. government as have Iranians.

This level of hostility is not due to economic burdens, lack of education among the Iranian American community (Emami 2014), or other factors that stereotypically cause discrimination against some groups; rather, it is political and ideological. Tehran might be right—Persian is the new Black; I should perhaps add Black at a time when some Black and Brown people were forced to pass as white to be safe and to be taken seriously as scholars, intellectuals, lawyers, politicians, or even in our held spiritual beliefs, whatever they might be.

Several Obama-era policies that eased economic sanctions on Iran helped generate more positive public sentiment toward Iran (Sanger 2016). However, these sentiments did not last, as the Trump administration instituted a travel ban on Iranian citizens (Executive Order No. 13780, 2017). Although Iran is not the only country on the travel ban list, this policy continues the general trend in U.S. policies regarding Iran over the last forty years and produces further isolation of Iranian people who come to the United States to flee the oppressive regime and lack of economic opportunities, to visit their families, or to seek medical care. Banning from travel a population that has never been involved in any terroristic activity in the United States is nothing other than political hatred, and it creates further division among people. This is fueled by the Republican Party's narrative of Iran as a nuclear threat in the most recent years. In response, to protect themselves, some Iranian Americans westernize their names or distance themselves from their Iranian culture and identity to blend in (to pass). Others create extensive support communities and work to avoid interactions with the non-Iranian community, even though the latter is not conducive to attending university, going to school, or working in the public sector ("Iranian Americans" 2014, 6)

Since the Iran hostage crisis, a new generation of American children has been born and some have reached adulthood. Many may be unaware of the hostage crisis and hold generally positive perceptions of Iran, but it seems neither Trump nor Hollywood would have it this way. In 2012, the movie *Argo* appeared to remind us all that Iranians are not the nice people you see in America; they are the fanatical, crazy, uncivilized people you see in the film. *Argo* "begins in November 1979, with the storming of the American Embassy in Tehran. A crowd breaks into the compound, taking more than fifty Americans hostage. Six escape through the back of the building and take refuge in the residence of the Canadian Ambassador" (Lane 2012). The movie is the tale of how these six Americans were able to escape Iran. Regardless of the film's factual accuracy, it gave the post-1979 generation a picture of the hostage crisis and taught them to fear Iranians all over again. At about the same time, the *Bravo* television series *Shahs of Sunset* aired for the first time. According to the Internet Movie Database, the series depicts "a group of affluent young Persian-American friends who juggle their flamboyant, fast-paced L.A. lifestyles with the demands of their families and traditions" ("Internet Movie Database" n.d.). *Shahs of Sunset* presents the other side of the *Argo* coin. It perpetuates similar stereotypes in a different environment, one in which Iranian people have room to express their individuality. The series depicts my community as being materialistic, shallow, emotionally unstable, judgmental, sexually promiscuous, self-absorbed, and obsessed with appearances. *Argo* and *Shahs of Sunset* are both relatively new (2012) media representations of Iranians and Iranian Americans, and they both aired two decades after the film *Not Without My Daughter*. Based on the autobiography of Betty Mahmoody, *Not Without My Daughter* tells a story that starts when Mahmoody, an American woman who was married to an Iranian physician, agreed to visit Iran with him in 1984. Shortly after their arrival, her husband told her that they were not going back to the United States. Mahmoody and her young daughter, Mahtob, eventually escape (Canby 1991). Although Mahmoody suffered abuse and confinement in Iran, she also had positive experiences, especially the warm welcome from her husband's family. I saw the movie in the theatre with my mother when it first came out in 1991. Despite the film's inaccuracies, I felt ashamed. I wanted to disappear out of the movie theatre without being seen, but no such luck! We were quite visible. The movie created a renewed mistrust towards men who were from Iran, the Middle East, or really any country that experienced unrest. Ever since, many white women in bicultural marriages have feared for their children's safety. I have heard this from their adult children whom I meet at conferences. Many were kept away from their Middle Eastern fathers because their mothers feared that their fathers might abuse them physically or emotionally or prevent them from seeing and knowing their American family members.

Not Without My Daughter appeared the year that I graduated from high school, nearly three years after I had arrived with my family in the United States. My college years started in the space between the hostage crisis and *Not Without My Daughter,* which eventually evolved into the triangle of *Argo*, *Shahs of Sunset,* and *Not Without My Daughter*. My "Americanization" experience has given me these confounding boundaries. It is in this space where I started college at the University of Oklahoma. A well-meaning colleague recently told me that I was "the right shade of brown," but that's not how I felt during my college years; quite the opposite. I found myself just the wrong shade of brown; unlike my colleague's perception of my social position to possess the ability to fit in many communities, I did not fit anywhere. It was not only the color of my skin but also the culture that I brought to the university with me.

I was the first person in my family to move away from home and live in a college dormitory at such a young age, except for the two who had come to the United Sates before the revolution to attend university. My departure from home elicited a family conflict: my father wished me well and my mother did not want me to leave the house. So, by moving away to college, I was not only moving to an unknown place where my identity was questioned and challenged, but I was also forced into a position that did not allow me to make a mistake. Any failure would have shown that my mother had been right in wanting me to stay home. Little did I know that the struggle of identity, assimilation, acculturation, and the lack of opportunity to fail would become a lifelong journey. Any failure would reflect badly not only on me, but also on the Iranian community. These have become the boundaries within which I have to live, grow, overcome negative social stereotypes, and flourish both personally and professionally.

THE OUTSIDER WITHIN

The experiences that I relayed in the last section are not mine alone. Many in the Iranian American community share these same kinds of experiences (Mobasher 2012; Maghbouleh 2017). Although we maintain the status of outsiders, the prospect of going "home" is neither realistic nor pleasant. So, we are people who bridge two cultures, stuck between acceptance and rejection. No matter which culture we are experiencing at any moment, we always have a foot in the other world. It is like living on a bridge and in "in-between worlds" that sometimes do not intercept (Ortega 2016; Lugones 1987). Living in that space full of uncertainties, contradictions, and dichotomies creates a sense of anxiety about whether we can be the kind of person who can function in that space or not. The *in-between* world for Iranian Americans, the life in the triangle, comes with contradictory languages, customs, priorities, foods, as well as contradictory life expectations. Gloria Anzaldua expresses this challenge as both anxiety-inducing and paralyzing (2007). Living as an immigrant comes with these challenges regardless of the political climate, but the Iranian American community lives in the triangle, a space saturated with negative sociopolitical sentiments and less-than-ideal relations between the two countries. This space requires walking on eggshells.

As Ortega (2016) reminds us, there exists an intimate relationship between the self and the world. Identity is never solidified. It is fluid and changes as the path of one's life changes. Iranian American immigrants have to display a certain flexibility and tolerance for change in order to create ourselves over and over again in a world that does not accept, appreciate, tolerate, nor value our existence. Along with living in an unfamiliar land, we develop the anxiety that accompanies trying to become the *right* kind of person, both for ourselves and for our new home. Living among abundant negative stereotypes makes this transition a lifelong project, one that evokes self-doubt, self-loathing, and a fragile sense of pride.

Self-hatred

Regardless of where we are in the spectrum of "assimilation," I often hear my fellow Iranian Americans talk about how much they do not like our community or its traditions. When I hear this, it seems to me that they are saying that they would rather be white, and not have to carry the burdens of Iranian (non-white) traditions, foods, accent, and holidays, and would rather be away from the family members who speak with an accent and behave in ways that are different than the majority culture. Regardless of the meaning behind their words, this has always been a difficult conversation for me. I detect a sense of self-hatred or at best a sense of unease. This feeling of discomfort, regardless of its strength, explains why some Iranian Americans identify as white and make every attempt to assimilate, especially publicly. Rejection of their Iranian identity is a rejection of me. I am aware that their self-identity is not about me or my personal journey, yet it feels personal. Not only do I feel judged embracing my Iranian-ness, I feel I am losing an ally, a friend, and that my community (hence safety net) is shrinking. Adrian Piper (1992) puts it well when she says that forgiving her "passing family members" has been one of the most difficult ethical challenges she has experienced.

It is difficult for Iranian Americans with non-European names and physical features to pass as white, but many Iranian Americans aim for assimilation into whiteness. Learning to be white, and becoming white, takes priority over their families and their families' traditions. This experience is painful both for those attempting to become white and for the family members and friends from whom they distance themselves. The emptiness they leave behind cannot be filled; it resembles death, the death of connection, even the death of a loved one. Intimate connections with people and environment are disrupted not only by immigration, but also by losing the people who connect us to our country of origin and are part of the human experience that formed our identity. Their rejection of culture is a rejection of us. We are left in a space in which we must try to accept the path they have chosen, mourn their loss and ours, and fill the hole created in our own sense of self. When they change the rules of the game, our world changes and we cease to know what to do or how to relate to the new rules. To do so, we must learn the culture of "non-Iranian" Iranians. As Iranians we know how to greet each other. We have been taught it all our lives, but the *passing* Iranian Americans ("the non-Iranian Iranians") don't play with those rules. It is unclear what their expectations are. There is a sense of anxiety about whether to acknowledge them in public, and (if we do acknowledge them) in which language to greet them (English or Persian), and which cultural mannerisms to employ. The simple act of greeting an Iranian American person who is white-passing by choice, thus becomes a challenge. Do I shake hands, hug them, kiss them (as we greet each other by kissing on both cheeks of those of the same gender)? These anxieties are not explicitly forced, but the implicit social messages are clear.

Living in the in-between worlds and in the borders between cultures comes with a feeling of isolation and shame resulting from the negative stereotypes concerning us and our community. We might even feel that we deserve to be stereotyped, and hence self-stereotype. Assimilation does not ease the shame and loathing; they become a part of our being. Liberation from self-stereotyping does not occur unless the individual becomes self-aware enough to overcome the negative social stereotypes against them. Even then, the struggle continues. The harsh realities of our lived experiences are woven into the fabric of the society in which we live; they are part of the air we breathe.

We linger in the space between, on the one hand, oppression engendered by stereotypical images and ideologies, and, on the other hand, quiet assimilation to avoid stereotypes and gain social and economic benefits. The process is uncertain, long, and self-alienating. Overcoming stereotypes is an act of self-discovery that requires us to tolerate painful experiences, to acknowledge the negativity, and to embrace many challenges generated by the intersection of our identities. As the number and complexity of our identities increase, the negative stereotypes that we face multiply, as does the harm that they cause. Society-wide stereotypes about a group have a significant effect on those who experience them. It is, therefore, worthwhile to spend the next section discussing stereotyping.

STEREOTYPING

Stereotyping is generally defined as overgeneralization; that is, taking a set of characteristics about some individuals in a population and assuming that the whole population shares these characteristics. Katherine Puddifoot (2017, 140), defines stereotyping as

> making a *judgment* about an individual that is influenced by a mental state associating members of a group, to which that individual belongs, more strongly than members of other groups with particular attributes, in virtue of their perceived social group membership. (Emphasis added.)

Although judgments based on stereotypes are sometimes accurate, stereotyping nevertheless has potentially grave consequences. We would be mistaken to talk about stereotypes merely as "judgments." Stereotyping is, as mentioned earlier, overgeneralization. Generalization is different from stereotyping in that generalizations (or judgments) are relatively easy to overcome. On the other hand, in the case of stereotyping, even when presented with the facts the stereotyper is unwilling to give up their beliefs. For example, in an interview a woman who supported the Trump administration's Muslim ban asserted that "they are mass murderers." When the interviewer repeatedly told her that mass murderers are typically white men, the woman said that she does not believe the research and will not change her mind, because she *knows* that Muslims are mass murderers. This is a classic case of stereotyping, showing that stereotypes are not easily abandoned. It requires conscious actions and responses to overcome stereotyping.

Even if we do not hold the common stereotypes about a certain group of people, we all know them. Lawrence Blum (2004, 252) explains stereotyping as follows;

> When we say that group X is stereotyped in a certain way, or that 'there is a stereotype of group X,' we generally refer to the recognizable presence in a certain sociocultural context of salient images of that group—more precisely, of associations between a group label and a set of characteristics. In this sense, stereotypes are cultural entities, widely held by persons in the culture or society in question, and widely recognized by persons who may not themselves hold the stereotype.

Stereotypes are either socially or individually learned. The former refers to stereotypes that are prevalent in our society and which we learn from others. We form the latter, however, as a result of our experiences with a group of people (Blum 2004, 254–255). By virtue of living in the same society, individuals know the stereotypes about both themselves and other people. We cannot help but learn sociocultural aspects of our world, as we grow up with them all around us. The very process of learning our culture's ideas about race and racism while growing up, is similar to learning our first language (Taylor 2013). Naturally, when we are children, we do not reflect much on what we learn about race, and we do not question the stereotypes we learn. However, this is not to absolve us of responsibility for our beliefs. Although we cannot help learning about stereotypes, as we grow into adulthood and develop the capacity for self-reflection, we become responsible if we allow stereotypes to take the place of reason and to affect our behavior.

Exposure to stereotyping has grave consequences for those who hold them. It can "cause epistemic mistakes: false beliefs and unreliable judgements. It is also associated with serious moral and political evils, including discrimination, and oppression" (Beeghly 2015). This is present in the killing of African American men and women as well as other social ills that stem from discriminatory beliefs (Yancy 2017; Zack 2015).

Stereotypes and stereotyping are involved in the kind of "cognitive distortions" that are also a part of "moral distortions" (Blum, 271). These distortions affect the way we respond to people who are negatively stereotyped, which in turn leads to negative consequences for them and their lives. Negative stereotypes can go so far as to blame people for their own misfortunes. Judith Howard (1984, 271) points out that

> Stereotypes influence our reaction to members of these [negatively stereotyped] groups. Those who subscribe to the stereotypes of young black men as aggressive and hostile, for example, may attribute the unemployment of a particular young black man to his presumed hostile disposition, ignoring current economic circumstances.

Consequently, the institutional oppression that the African American population experiences goes unnoticed and unaddressed. Iranian Americans are similarly stereotyped. A recent study on the perceptions of Middle Eastern men, by Negin Ghavami and Letitia Ann Peplau (2012), found that they are stereotyped as being suspicious and holding anti-West attitudes. This sentiment, coupled with the perception of Middle Easterners as terrorist Muslim fundamentalists (or really, just Muslims), as well as former president George W. Bush's announcement naming Iran the "axis of evil," leaves Iranian American people in a socially, politically, and personally difficult situation (Bush 2002). Being at the receiving end of stereotypes is both emotionally and politically challenging.

Harms of Stereotypes and Stereotyping

It is safe to say, as Erin Beeghly (2015, 688) does, that we may have to be "pluralist" in the way we view problems with stereotyping. That is, there is no single way to explain the wrongs of stereotyping. Stereotyping is wrong because it denies one's individuality, ignores individual values, makes monolithic generalizations about groups of individuals, makes moral judgments about individuals before interacting with them, and is alienating, dehumanizing, and dangerous. Beeghly also points out the multitude of ways in which we can cause harm through stereotyping: in communicating, in behavior, in employment decisions, and in our own thoughts when we come into contact with individuals who belong to stereotyped groups (680–684). But all of these modes have one underlying commonality: categorizing all people based on their group membership and applying that categorization to every individual whom we perceive as belonging to that group. She gives an example: "A woman might whisper to a friend—'Persians [majority Iranian ethnic group] are such materialists'—as they pass a Persian woman in Beverly Hills bedecked in designer clothing" (682). This is an example of stereotyping, and one that I have mentioned in the discussion of *Shahs of Sunset*. Although she claims that this stereotype is only in communication, it is not without consequences for her interactions with Persians. Although materialism is a deeply American trait, calling someone "materialistic" connotes judgments of shallowness, untrustworthiness, insincerity, and even a lack of integrity. If approached to conduct business with Persians, this woman might be hesitant to proceed, believing that Persians are untrustworthy because money is their primary motive. Taken by itself, the woman's comment on Persians being materialistic is not a grave case of stereotyping, nor is it a particularly harmful one. However, the web of oppression is made of many threads that create a cage, using Marilyn Frye's (1983) metaphor.

Stereotyping is a social phenomenon perpetuated by those who hold overgeneralized and faulty beliefs about groups they perceive to be "other." But it also leads to self-stereotyping. Those who are negatively stereotyped internalize the stereotypes, and their negative mindset becomes a limiting factor in the ways they conduct their lives (Reynolds, Oakes, Haslam, Nolan, and Dolnik 2000). The internalization of stereotypes leads to psychological oppression, which occurs when the victim becomes what the oppressor expects them to become. Research shows that society-wide negative stereotypes against a group have a huge influence on the way that the stereotyped group members see themselves (Jost and Banaji 1994). Quite often, we internalize the negative stereotypes against us and experience, consciously or not, a level of self-shame—we feel ashamed of being that kind of person, whether or not the stereotypes apply to us as individuals. One vivid memory in my life is when an Iranian woman told me that I should be glad that my daughter, who is much fairer than I in complexion, is "white" because "white kids are smarter and more polite than non-white kids." The woman who said this to me is not white, and neither am I. Her statement is pregnant with self-shame. As Sandra Bartky (1990, 30) puts it, "many oppressed persons come to regard themselves as uniquely unable to satisfy normal criteria of psychological health or moral adequacy. To believe that my inferiority is a function of the kind of person I am may make me ashamed of being of *this* kind." I carry this self-shame into all walks of my life. Internalizing the inferior social status, I feel ashamed to be the kind of person who has these negative stereotypes about them. Self-shame is a hindrance to one's life options. Putting it in Martha Nussbaum's (2001) terms, self-shame can lead to limiting one's development of capabilities, which results in affirming stereotypes against one's group.

Consider the case of Iranian Americans. We share with our host country (the United States) a social and political history that has been tainted by four decades of animosity on both sides. A prevalent view of Iranian people as untrustworthy and unwelcome has resulted from many factors. Among them are the images of violent Iranians that came across our television screens starting during the Iran hostage crisis, and the anti-Iranian laws that were passed following the hostage crisis. Another factor is the "Iranian Jim Crow" of the 1970s and 1980s, a term that refers to the laws that were made after the Iran hostage crisis that excluded Iranians from many facets of the society (Mobasher 2012). Reflected among the harms of these stereotypes are Howard's findings that stereotypes affect the way we react to the misfortunes of groups that are negatively stereotyped (1984). We blame the victims of discrimination for their victimization. Consider the following example.

After my father had made on-time rental payments for fifteen years for the business location he rented, where he ran a restaurant, the landowners refused to renew his lease. In his late sixties and not quite ready to retire, my father had to close his restaurant and find a new way to make a living. Instead of recognizing the landowners' action as a display of discrimination and racism, many people questioned my father, trying to find a reason that *made sense to them* for the landowner's refusal to renew the lease. They wondered if he had paid his rent payments on time, if he had disruptive clients, or if perhaps the landowners wanted to do something else with the property. Yet as I write this, four years later, the property is still empty and up for rent. My father had paid his rent on time and was willing to accept a rent increase. His customers were generally "respectable" and non-disruptive: mostly students and faculty of the nearby health sciences campus of the University of Oklahoma and the employees of several government offices and local non-governmental organizations. My father had not done anything to cause his lease to be terminated, nor could he do anything to stop it from happening. Such is the nature of racism and holding to one's deep-seated stereotypes. The landowners, a prominent Oklahoma City family, did not want to rent to an Iranian American immigrant. The messages of hatred that they had heard about the Iranian people fogged their judgment towards doing business with one, even if it meant losing the chance to collect the monthly rent. My father lost his $250,000 business in his late sixties and had to start over in a new career.

This is merely one example of the sorts of events that commonly result from the "cognitive distortions" that we need to consider when discussing stereotyping. Although recent years have seen more frequent discussion of the moral implications of stereotyping (Beeghly 2015, 251), Blum is correct in stating that the "cognitive distortions involved in stereotyping lead to various forms of moral distortion, to which moral philosophers have paid inadequate attention." The psychological oppression caused by stereotyping is morally reprehensible in two ways. First, it ignores one's agency and needs; second, it threatens one's development of an authentic self and self-determination (Bartky 1990, 24). Claude Steele's research on stereotype threat, discussed in the next section, further explains the consequences of society-wide negative stereotypes about a group.

Stereotype Threat

According to Steele (1999), widespread negative stereotypes against one's group leads to stereotype threat. That is, those who are negatively (or positively) stereotyped are always under the threat of being watched to see if they indeed conform to the stereotypes. Blum (2004, 287) adds:

> the harm caused by stereotypes operating in the mode of stereotype threat is not dependent on a specific stereotyper or, more generally, an agent of stereotyping.

> Stereotype threat depends on two conditions . . . an awareness of the cultural stereotype, and a situational activation that heightens consciousness of the stereotype in the moment.

Unlike Bartky, Steele does not believe that stereotyped individuals internalize the stereotypes, but he asserts that their anxiety about stereotype threat adds an external challenge that is the cause of poor performance in certain circumstances, including standardized testing and college classrooms.

Claude Steele and Joshua Aronson (1995, 797) found that "the existence of such stereotypes means that anything one does or any of the one's features that conform to it make the stereotype more plausible as a self-characterization in the eyes of others, and perhaps even in one's own eyes." The stereotyped individual develops anxiety about whether they are perpetuating the stereotypes, or perhaps they see themseves as the stereotypes. We might fit some of the stereotypes about ourselves, but stereotypes are formed not as the characteristics of all members of a group, but as the *perceived* characteristics of a group. Hence, sometimes those stereotypes apply to individuals, but stereotyping is the application of characteristics to *all* members of the stereotyped group. The challenge of performance for the stereotyped person is not to fit *any* of the stereotypes, because of the worry that those behaviors, however small, will imply that they fit the other stereotypes as well. I discussed the stereotypes regarding Iranian American people at the beginning of this chapter. We mingle in the space between two extremes (vices), greed and fundamentalism. Even though I live a modest life as a single mother working in academia, I worry that my indulgences will send the message of greed and that my political participation in marches or criticism of the government tags me as fundamentalist, anti-American, and somehow scary. My behavior can further stereotype other members of the Iranian American community.

As a Iranian American woman of color, I live under a microscope. My most miniscule acts that correspond to the stereotypes perpetuate the negative stereotypes against me and my community, because everything we do speaks for our whole community. These pressures come with an emotional cost. These emotional distresses, at the least, contribute to poor performace, which further perpetuates the stereotypes.

As history shows, the harms of stereotyping are not merely emotional. Slavery was justified by questioning the humanity of African people; the violence against indigenous populations was justified by classifying them as "uncivilized"; and Mexican Americans are categorized by the most powerful man in the country as "rapists, criminals, and drug dealers" (Reilly 2016). Iranian American people have been denied jobs, banned from restaurants, and subjected to ridicule and unfounded fear (Mobasher 2012). Much of this stems from the Islamic revolution in 1979 and the hostage crisis in

1979–1981. The dehumanization and economic harms caused by stereotyping stem from a disregard for Iranian Americans' humanity and ways of life. We live in the boundary between celebrating human rights and being denied "adequate agency, autonomy, and cultural expression" (Baily and Cuomo 2008, 11).

It is in this space that we (the Iranian American people) live, grow, create our identities, raise our children, work, go to school, teach, and love, all the while wondering whether they really belong. Marginalized populations constantly wonder whether we really belong. Immigrants—those on the borderlands living on the bridge between two worlds—must struggle their way out of one world, sometimes a safe one that welcomes them and where they know the rules and have abundant support, and learn to participate in another world that is sometimes hostile and unwelcoming. Living in this space, experiencing negative stereotypes about one's identity, has a significant effect on the people that we become and the way we identify as individuals and members of a society. The development of one's identity in this space is the focus of the next section.

Identity and Stereotyping in "In-Between Worlds"

Anzaldua (2017) addresses the anxiety that a person experiences when they are branded *the other* and fall through the cracks of the social structure. In that space, we ought to develop our sense of self, but this is a challenge for those of us who live in multiple worlds. This is the result of what Maria Lugones (1987, 10) calls "being in between worlds." She describes the "world" as follows:

> A "world" in my sense may be an actual society given its dominant culture's description and construction of life, including a construction of the relationships of production, of gender, race, etc. But a "world" can also be such a society given a non-dominant construction. . . . A "world" need not be a construction of a whole society. It may be a construction of a tiny portion of a particular society. It may be inhabited by just a few people. Some "worlds" are bigger than others.

I live in at least two worlds, both of which I know quite well: one in which I was raised, the Iranian world, and one that I adopted, the American world. The former set the base of my being, and the latter became my place of living. Neither feels like home or, as bell hooks calls it, the "homeplace" where

> one could freely confront the issue of humanization, where we could resist . . . where all black [marginalized] people could strive to be subjects, not objects,

where we could be affirmed in our minds and hearts despite poverty, hardship, and deprivation, where we could restore to ourselves the dignity denied us on the outside in the public world. (384)

Neither Iran nor the United States feels like the kind of homeplace that hooks describes here. I am an *Americanized Iranian.* I lived in different worlds in Iran: a secular one at home and a repressive Islamic one outside. Now I live in different worlds in the United States: an academic one, a personal multicultural one, and one that sometimes denies my dignity and value. I travel in and out of all these worlds often, sometimes daily.

Lugones (1987, 11) defines "travel" the act of shifting from "being one person to being a different person." We move in and out of those worlds that might be radically different from one another with expert fluidity. Those of us who "travel" in multiple worlds will have different expectations, foods, cultural behaviors, friendships, and possibly languages, as I do. There are often no harsh barriers because we are well versed in living in two worlds. However, the experience is, as Anzaldua also notes, anxiety-inducing. We do not know if we are doing the right thing in the right way. We fear that being stereotyped in the dominant world jeopardizes our sense of integrity, because we do not behave according to a unified sense of self—there is no unity—but rather according to fluid borders, our identities sitting next to each other as would a pack of cells occupying a common space in one's body. Our identity as "a pack of cells" represents the fact that our sense of self is fragmented into parts, some of which would appear in some *worlds* and not others. In what comes next, I will discuss the challenge of having a "unified" sense of self while engaging in "world traveling" on a regular basis.

INTEGRITY AND IDENTITY

On the face of it, our ordinary sense of integrity requires that we behave in the ways that we believe we *should* behave (Rivera 2007). For this reason, what we feel, think, say, and do all have to match up, and we also ought to have an integrated sense of self. According to John Cottingham (2010, 3), integrity is the "idea that I have a 'true identity,' a unified, integrated self, the self I am meant to be, the self that expresses all that is best and most distinctive about me—and the goal of my life should be, as it were, to grow into that unified self." This definition of integrity, which is *integrity as self-integration,* is slightly different from Lisa Rivera's definition. Cottingham's sense of integrity speaks of a reflective self-realization but does not address how we make this happen. Cottingham acknowledges that this might be too much to pack into the concept of "integrity," but he is committed to this dense idea of integrity. Damian Cox, Marguerite La Caze, and Michael Levine (2017) add that the "view of integrity as maintenance of identity-conferring commitments recognizes the relevance of self-knowledge to *acting* with integrity. If people fail to act on their core commitments, through self-deception, weakness of will, cowardice, or even ignorance, then to this extent they may be said to lack integrity" (para. 20).

I agree with both of these notions about creating a wholly integrated sense of identity, but I also worry about the moral implication of this sense of integrity in situations where one cannot safely express one's personal identity, or where these expressions come with a penalty. Our integrity is violated not only by our own actions that are contrary to our life goals and dispositions, but also by the oppressive social institutions that penalize us for displaying our authentic selves. Although the integration of self is a necessary component of being an authentic person, the complexities of life and certain oppressive situations may prevent one from achieving self-integration, or at least *expressing* one's sense of self-integration, which I hold to be necessary to authenticity. Lack of self-integration may be caused by lack of life experiences, lack of the necessary tools for self-reflection, or life traumas, or it could be due to multiplicity of the self (Lugones 1987; Ortega 2016; Anzaldua 2007). Perhaps acknowledging the lack of self-integration is adequate for having integrity and also authenticity.

Authenticity, as in the case of integrity, requires self-reflection. As Michele Moses (2000, 297) puts it,

> a sense of authenticity is characterized by the ability to be true to oneself. This can occur in two ways. First, one's feeling of authenticity stems from the inside, from inner reflection upon one's personal identity. Second, it stems also from one's relations with others. This second way that authenticity is shaped is fundamentally *dialogical* in nature, and the public recognition of one's worth is a key component. (Emphasis added.)

When it comes to my racial, ethnic, and national identities, I have no doubt as to what they are. Cultural minorities who find themselves on a bridge between two cultures know their struggles and the dichotomies with which they are presented. Our challenges to living an authentic life typically stem from the second aspect that Moses describes, "the public recognition of one's worth." We live in a society that it is racially hierarchical. Some groups have been granted more value than others. The Trump administration has clearly shown us that the lives of Iranians do not matter. I cannot separate myself from the Iranians in Iran. My connection to that community, my place of birth and home for the first fifteen years of my life, is very much a part of me. Some current news and my experiences of racist behaviors towards my community have indicated that many of my fellow citizens are not very fond of Iranians either. So, it might seem to be not only prudent, but also logical, to hide that identity (the one we have developed, and with which we identify, internally) from the majority community. So, many Iranian Americans aim to assimilate and deny our culture publicly. Some use this assimilation to change the system. By becoming "white" and adopting the majority culture's habits, they gain greater social capital and are therefore more likely to be heard when calling for social change. In essence, they are empowered to change the system from within, because they are no longer seen mainly as outsiders. However, others who assimilate do not attempt to change the culture; instead, they support the status quo.

Besides our familial obligations, there are two reasons that minority populations do not engage in changing the system. First, society pushes them to the margins by creating an exclusive and difficult-to-cross barrier that they must traverse before being allowed to participate in the political dialogue. Some feel too intimidated to engage in a community whose rules they did not participate in making. Second, those on the margins of society, such as immigrants and multiracial or multicultural individuals, recognize their status and, mostly, tread with caution. To deconstruct this a bit, we must discuss, at the least, epistemic injustice, multiculturalism, self-oppression, poverty, lack of resources, and stereotype threat, among other factors that affect human behavior. Each of these components could very well be a reason preventing people from actively engaging in self-government; it is not due to lack of interest, integrity, or authenticity. Moses (2000, 295) adds that self-determination, as well as authenticity, depend on "a favorable social context of choice," which is certainly missing in our society. She asserts:

> When choices are made under conditions of inequality and oppression, we may doubt their authenticity. So, while these types of choices may not be directly coerced choices, they are made from within a severely limited range of options. It is the character of the choice that makes a difference. Individuals are certainly responsible for their choices, but an unjust situation arises when there are grave inequalities within the context from which certain people are making their life choices. (296)

The oppressive and unequal circumstances affect the manifestations of choices and push individuals to make choices they might not have made were their circumstances not oppressive. This means that a person could very well be true to themselves in their *beliefs and thoughts*, but still not find the social safety to *behave* in ways that are authentic. It is true that I would rather live in a world where my identity, as well as all others' identities, are not only tolerated but also accepted and celebrated. The human situation is permeated with inequalities: both the inequalities that people are born with, such as differing visual acuity and height, and those that are completely socially constructed. I have touched on only one aspect of the sense of self in relation to authenticity, but there are countless others within and among individuals. As we develop theories and judgments, our philosophical understanding of authenticity and integrity must recognize this.

Those of us who are first-generation immigrants *do* have divided identities, as well as multiple racial maps that we navigate (Haslanger 2005; Mills 1998). As William Cross (1991, 214) puts it, "one's identity is a maze or map that functions in a multitude of ways to guide and direct exchanges with one's social and material realities." We have to navigate sometimes radically different maps. We have to learn both maps very well, or we will get lost or left behind. Trying to pass, or assimilate, does not violate our sense of integrity or authentic self.

Integrity and authenticity both are matters of degree, and they might even operate differently on different maps. One can be authentic on some maps and not others. Ortega, Lagunos, and Anzaldua give us adequate explanations of these cases. Those of us who travel between worlds do not have the luxury of having only one self, or of navigating only one map or maze. We operate in different worlds. The standards, expectations, cultural norms, borders, and paths are multiple, and navigating different maps requires us to use different aspects of our selves. Furthermore, my navigating skills might be uneven with regard to different aspects of the map. For instance, I might be better able to navigate my moral commitments than my social commitments. So, in my relations to morality, I act with integrity and in ways that are authentic to me. However, given my "precarious" social status, I might not know the best way of simply "being." In that situation, passing, assimilating, and denying parts of my cultural identity are not detrimental to my sense of integrity, nor are they compromising to my authenticity, given that I am aware of the uncertainties in my relations with the external world. As Kwame Anthony Appiah (2004) puts it, the most authentic we can become is within our fractured identities. As he says, we ought to "live with fractured identities; engage in identity play; find solidarity, yes, but recognize contingency, and, above all, practice irony." It turns out that it is morally okay to have our fractured identities and live our fractured existences.

CHAPTER SUMMARY

The effects of society-wide negative stereotypes about a group have been studied in many disciplines, especially psychology and sociology, and have been backed up by experimental data. This body of research sheds light on the situation of Iranian Americans. Since the hostage crisis, we have witnessed a significant campaign, both politically and socially, in the mass media and among some political leaders, to create a negative perception of this population. We, Iranian Americans, try to become Americanized in any way we possibly can to blend in, in order to avoid the stereotypes about us. Some ways of blending in are meant to create a sense of comfort both in us and in the people around us, as well as to gain greater acknowledgment of our humanity.

When I speak about "blending in," my reference is not toward blending in with just any culture in the United States. Blending in with other marginalized communities is not quite as challenging as blending in with the white mainstream culture. Iranian Americans and other marginalized communities share many cultural, social, and political elements, some of which do not fit in with the mainstream society. Sometimes our physical appearances help us pass as white and benefit from the privileges, but there are also challenges associated with passing. Passing people suffer from the effects of negative stereotypes towards the members of the group with whom they identify, regardless of their perceived identity. The next chapter will dive deeper into this topic and identify the ways that race and ethnicity figure into the discussion.

Chapter Two

What Are You?

A Discussion on Race, Ethnicity, and (Iranian) Identity

BACKGROUND STORY

Several factors have contributed to my desire to explore the idea of race: as mentioned in the last chapter, my "Americanization" process in the boundaries formed by *Argo, Shahs of Sunset*, and *Not Without My Daughter;* my experiences as a woman of color in academia; and the direct and indirect messages I've received from multiple sources telling me to pass as Greek or hide my ethnicity in other ways. In addition to those, there is a sense of curiosity about the difference between race and ethnicity that moved me. When I was filling out the job application for my first lecturer position in philosophy at the University of Texas Pan American campus, I came to the race/ethnicity question. There were the usual options, as well as two I had not seen before: Mexican white and Mexican Black. These terms refer to a combination of one's nationality and race, which is not common in the United States; the mixing of race and nationality was not present for any other group of people. I am generally racialized as Mexican, and my daughter, who is "white-passing," struggles to earn her identity. I use the term "earn" here because her identity as Iranian American is often denied her.

My daughter is biracial (her father is white), and she identifies as a person of color. I heard many chuckles when my daughter, at age twelve, expressed her identity as though she had been expressing a case of "mistaken identity." In her experience, neither her biology nor her skin color determines her ethnic identity. Her identity has evolved around mostly first generation Iranian American immigrants. She hears different languages at home, celebrates both Iranian and American holidays, and often eats food that most Americans do not eat at home, if ever. My daughter has strong connections with her Iranian American family members and knows relatively little about her white relatives. So, she identifies as Iranian American, but she passes as white due to her physical appearance. It is in this context that I come to explore race, ethnicity, and the process by which people become racialized.

The following goals drive my interest in race theory. First, I hope to explain the nature of race in a way that strengthens the fight against racial injustices. Our theory of race must help us achieve that goal. Second, and more personally, I want to know what it means for me, for my daughter, and for the community that shares our identity when I say that I am Persian, Brown, white, Iranian, and so on. To this aim, I will discuss theories of race and explore how the Iranian American racial identity presents itself.

BACKGROUND ON RACE AND ETHNICITY

"Race" is a politically charged term, especially at a time in which we are experiencing backlash against liberal social justice movements. Following the 2016 U.S. presidential election, when Donald Trump was named president-elect, people of color started experiencing this backlash. The election results shook people whose identities were attacked during the campaign. After the 2016 election, the future of marginalized people was not a continuation of what the Obama administration had promoted. The progress of the previous eight years was gradually undone, and the mainstream society's acceptance of certain identities began to decline. Our appearance and perceived identity, if not white, can make us targets of bullying and discrimination. This is nothing new. Historically, human rights violations based on skin color, appearance, or perceived identity have been justified by claims that certain groups are "inferior." Consider a recent case of the Sikh professor of religion at Trinity University in San Antonio who competed in the 2016 New York City Marathon. One runner told others in front of him to "run faster because 'that guy from ISIS' was chasing them" (Ramos 2016). The professor's perceived race made him the target for mocking and hateful speech. This is an example of racism, but it is also an example of racialization, the process whereby a particular race is "assigned" to a person based on their appearance. In this case, it also happens to be incorrect, as Sikhs are not Muslim. Philosophy of race scholars, with the help of scientists, have given us enough evidence to deny "racial essentialism," and the existence of race as a biological category. Although not a biological reality, race is socially real (Haslanger 2000, 43), and it plays a significant role in our society—economically, emotionally, psychologically, and also with regard to safety (Alcoff 1996). Racial categorizations, whatever they are, are also legally protected and used politically to divide groups (Lopez 1996).

Racializing has adverse effects on the wellbeing of those being racialized. Racialization is justified by racial essentialism, which is sometimes referred to simply as racialism. According to Ron Mallon (2004, 647),

> Racism is a moral and political concern since the presence of thick clusters of biologically determined character traits may provide a foundation for racist claims of racial moral, intellectual or cultural superiority . . . *racist* doctrines involve both the endorsement of racialism and additional claims of the superiority of one or another race. The ontological consensus undermines racism by undermining racialism.

I am committed to the *ontological consensus*. Ontological consensus denies the existence of universal and unchanging definitions of race. It also entails that racialists are mistaken about what races are. Racial skeptics (Zack 1993; Appiah 1985) and racial constructionists (Outlaw 1990, 1995, 1996; Mills 1998; Root 2000) also agree that racialism is false.

Racial categories are fluid and changing. The concept of race does not travel from one society to another, nor does it pick the right racial designation each time. What unites people as a racialized group is neither biology nor physical appearance, but rather their culture and shared history with their family. This reminds us of W. E. B. Du Bois's views on Black identity: "a collective black identity [is] based primarily on a shared history and culture, and only secondarily on a common biology" (Shelby 2002, 235).

In contrast to racial essentialism, racial constructivism is the notion that race, although not a metaphysical reality, is socially real. Race determines people's social status within hierarchies but is not an essential property of individuals. Unlike essentialist views, constructivist perspectives account for diversity within races, without dictating that our appearances or biology determine our culture, intelligence, moral disposition, or other characteristics. In this view, the concept of "race" is fluid and does not travel across time and place (Root 2000). People are racialized differently in different contexts. That is, an individual (or groups) could be racialized one way in one time and place, but not in another.

Sally Haslanger (2000, 33) distinguishes three approaches to studies of race: conceptual, descriptive, and analytical.

> A *conceptual* inquiry into race or gender would seek an articulation of our *concept* of race or gender. . . . In contrast to the conceptual project, a *descriptive* project is not concerned with exploring the nuances of our concepts . . . it focuses instead on their extension. The third sort of project takes an *analytical* approach. . . . On this approach the task is not to explicate our ordinary concepts;

nor is it to investigate the kind that we may or may not be tracking with our everyday conceptual apparatus; instead we begin by considering more fully the pragmatics of our talk employing the terms in question.

Like Haslanger, I propose an analytical approach, which allows us the use of both ordinary everyday use of the term "race" and racial designations, as well as empirical methods of investigating what race is, but does not limit us to just these methods. In the ordinary use of a term, Haslanger (2010) refers to a way that people use a term without really knowing or needing to have any knowledge of its essence. In the ordinary use of a term the knowledge of the term is "tacit" but the contextual use of a term is required to know the meaning of it. With the analytical approach, we can decide what race is by investigating how the terms are actually used and when it is appropriate to use them. The "world by itself can't tell us . . . it is up to us to decide what in the world, if anything" race is (Haslanger 2000, 34). Let us think through this with some examples.

Consider the confusing and ironic situation of Iranian American law professor John Tehranian. Tehranian (2009) applied for a job as a law professor and was turned down because the search committee was looking to increase faculty diversity. Tehranian was told that he was clearly white and male and they wanted to hire a person of color for this position. His white-passing appearance was used to determine his race as "white." Without further investigation he was mis-categorized with a group with whom he didn't identify. Tehranian's case is especially interesting because he faces discrimination for not being white, while he is also denied a job because he is white. Many of us living in between worlds experience such contradictions in our lives.

Most Iranians have similar experiences to Tehranian's when visiting Iran. Azadeh Moaveni, the Middle East correspondent for *Time* and author of the book *Lipstick Jihad: Being Iranian in America and American in Iran*, points out that despite living most of her life in the United States, she has always experienced life as being "the Iranian woman" (Moaveni 2007). However, when visiting Iran, she is "Amrikaee" (American). Regardless of your community, it is alienating to realize that even the community you identify with categorizes you as "not ours." We need a theory of race that captures this crossroads of racial identity. Given such experiences, and the significance of race in everyone's life, I will not deny the existence of race. Haslanger's view, which describes race as a social construction, resonates with me. She argues that people do not *have* a race but *are given* a race. One is racialized by one's bodily appearance and its perceived connection with a particular geographic area and, by virtue of this classification, one is harmed or benefited.

WHAT IS RACE?

We expect our concept of race to fulfill many functions. We want it to account for the phenomenon of passing, to not travel, and to be non-biological (Mallon 2004). Additionally, Haslanger lists four concerns that should guide the development of our conceptions about race. First, any conception of race should identify the inequalities between races and on what basis these inequalities continue. Second, our theory should recognize the similarities and differences between racial groups within a society. What does it mean when someone's race is white or Asian, or Black, or Persian? Third, it should give an account of what role, if any, race plays in an individual's art, religion, or philosophy. This concern will help answer my question of racial identity. Last, and perhaps most important, our theory of race should help us recognize everyone's agency and integrity. This is an important component of critical social theory, and it supports the development of a just and inclusive environment whose goal is inclusivity rather than mere diversity.

I want to be explicit and note that I will not endorse the essentialist (biological) view of race. However, I also wish to acknowledge that, although essentialism has been refuted by both scientists and social scientists, the attitudes toward and stereotypes regarding racial groups are still real. People do not usually characterize their stereotypical beliefs as being based on biology. Instead, they explain their beliefs as being based on the attitudes or dispositions that the stereotyped group is widely believed to possess. For instance, most people do not openly dispute the humanity of the African American population, but the mass incarceration of Black men and the murder of unarmed Black men and women tell a different story. Stereotypes of Black men as being dangerous, violent, lazy, unmotivated, or somehow unfit for our civilization are not defended based on their skin color but rather their current situation, whatever that might be (Darby 2006, 436-437). Black people are systematically disenfranchised, murdered at the hands of police, or locked away by the not-so-just justice system. This has unforeseen effects on the community's economic and emotional wellbeing as well as its physical health (Mitchell and Ronzio 2011; Gaylord-Harden, Noni, So, Bai, and Tolan 2017; Levy-Pounds 2013). These stereotypes and generalizations about Black men lead to our society's generally negative disposition about this group. Shelby (2002, 262) adds that

> The peculiar content of antiblack racist ideology (with its images of blacks as lazy, stupid, hypersexual, and disposed to acts of aggression), the enslavement and brutal treatment of Africans in the New World, and the subsequent exclusion of blacks from the mainstream of American civic and social life have com-

bined to give antiblack race prejudice a distinctive character among American forms of racism.

I agree with this characterization, and although my main focus in this book is not the African American community, I would be committing an offense if I failed to acknowledge both the African American and Native American communities in my race dialogue. Racism affects different communities in different ways, but every member of a marginalized community is affected by negative stereotypes against them or their identities. The essential characteristics that we assign to people, be they positive or negative, can be dangerous. For example, the "model minority" myth of Asian Americans asserts that they are especially successful, intelligent, and hardworking. Yet Asian American women hold the second highest suicide rate among minority groups, and a recent study claimed that this is due to the high expectations that are placed on them (Hahm, Gonyea, Chiao, Koritsanszky 2014).

The case of Iranian Americans poses a peculiar kind of challenge to the study of race and racism. The Iranian American community is generally well educated and affluent. But Iranian Americans who are not "white-passing" experience hostility, regardless of their socioeconomic status, education, or social standing. After the elections of 2016, the hostility has become more overt and is directed toward individuals who were born here and are well-assimilated as well as toward immigrants. As mentioned in chapter 1, the Iranian American identity is confined within the triangle between *Argo, Shahs of Sunset,* and *Not Without My Daughter.* If one is male and looks Middle Eastern, one is often perceived with suspicion. Our fellow citizens react with caution and fear in the presence of people who look Middle Eastern. It is in that space that we, Iranian Americans, struggle to humanize ourselves and to protect our children from the stereotypes that haunt us. Even children are not safe from harassment and emotional violence. My daughter, at the age of six, was told by a white American relative that the government is "watching you and your family because Iranians are terrorists." She didn't know what "terrorist" meant or why the government was watching us. In that moment, I experienced the feelings of pain expressed by Martin Luther King, Jr. (or any African American parent) when they have to explain racism to their young children, and its implications in their daily lives (1963). There is a special kind of sorrow that accompanies these kinds of conversations.

My daughter, whose "white-passing" appearance prompts her classmates to disbelieve her regarding her ethnic background, often experiences the denial of her identity. Although race is socially prescribed, identity has both a social and a psychological element to it. I will explore both of these elements in the remainder of this chapter, addressing the concept of ethnicity and how it helps us understand racial and ethnic identity, and how this understanding manifests itself in the Iranian American community.

Categories of Race

When studying race, we can take either an objective or a nonobjective approach. The objective approach "usually connotes the independence of what we choose, what we believe" when exploring the ideas of race (Mills 1998, 45), and ignores the personal, historical, social, and political aspects of race. Two theories take the objective approach: racial realism and racial constructivism.

Racial realism is the view that races are natural kinds. "A racial realist will also believe that the differences between races are not confined to the superficial morphological characteristics of skin color, hair type, and facial features, but extend to significant moral, intellectual, characterological, and spiritual characteristics also, that there are 'racial essences'" (Mills 1998, 48). In this definition of "racial realism," racial realists inevitably fall into the essentialist view of race. Racial essentialism claims that a person's physical traits are a reliable way to determine their abilities, characteristics, and culture. According to this view of race, just as we are born with a particular hair or skin color, we are born with certain kinds of intelligence, abilities, cultural attributes, or character traits that are essential to the race we are born into. For instance, Asians are smart and hardworking (the model minority); Mexicans are ignorant and dirty and, as president-elect Trump told the whole world throughout his campaign, "rapists and criminals"; Native Americans are drunks; Middle-Easterners are violent terrorists; and so forth. Essentialists would argue that these characteristics are inherent, a necessary feature of a person's very existence. According to the essentialist view, I, as an Iranian American woman, cannot be any other way than the stereotypes about me. Even if my path in life were different, I would still be the same person with the same qualities I have today, due to my biological makeup. The fact that I survived a revolution, war, and immigration would make no difference in my psychological makeup or abilities. Naturally, I find this description of race highly problematic. My skin color does not dictate my culture; my experiences do. My daughter does not suffer from the fears and anxieties that I experienced when I was her age (fifteen). Her life brings its own set of challenges and struggles. As a white-passing child of a first-generation Iranian American immigrant family, she experiences neither the racist behaviors that communities of color experience, nor the overt racism that I have experienced.

Just as my daughter has not experienced my traumas, white-passing people of color do not experience the same sort of trauma as their darker counterparts. Yet it does not follow that they are unaffected by discrimination, negative stereotypes, or the traumas that their communities have experienced in the past and continue to experience now. Native populations have spoken of how the generational trauma their ancestors experienced continues to affect them today (Walters, Mohammed, Evans-Campbell, Beltran, Chae, Duran 2011). African American clinical psychologist Joy DeGruy (2017) discusses post-slave trauma syndrome to argue that the trauma faced by African ancestors during the transcontinental slave trade continues to plague the African American population today. Traumas that are untreated for generations have an adverse effect on any population. On a much smaller scale, perhaps my daughter carries with her some of the trauma that I have experienced. I have passed my fears down to the next generation, and I am not alone. Iranian Americans continue to perpetuate their traumas through their trauma symptoms, as described by social learning theory (Bandura 1977). Social learning theory explains that we learn from our environment by observing and imitating behaviors and the responses to those behaviors. The transmission of these experiences ends up "looking like" our culture: the culture of the Iranian Americans, who survived revolution, war, and immigration, then experienced discrimination in their host countries, has been significantly affected by those experiences. For this reason, among others, we would be mistaken to accept the essentialist view of race.

Naomi Zack (2010), being an eliminativist about race reminds us that science has denied race as a biological category, and argues against the concept of race since it is not really a biological category. Although there are biological reasons for one's physical appearance, there are no other biologically interesting differences between people from different races:

> race is through and through a social construct, previously constructed by science, now by society, including its most extreme victims. But, *we cannot abandon race*, because people would still discriminate and there would be no nonwhite identities from which to resist. Also, many people just don't want to abandon race and they have a fundamental right to their beliefs. So, race remains with us as something that needs to be put right. (Zack 2014)

Likewise, Charles Mills and Sally Haslanger both point out that race is not "metaphysically" real, although it is socially real (Mills 1998; Haslanger 2000). As Mills explains,

> Race is not "metaphysical" in the deep sense of being eternal, unchanging, necessary, part of the basic furniture of the universe. But race is a *contingently* deep reality that structures our particular social universe, having a social objectivity and causal significance that arise out of *our* particular history. For racial realism, the social metaphysics is simply an outgrowth of a natural metaphysics; for

racial constructivism, there is no natural metaphysics, and the social metaphysics arises directly out of the social history. (48)

Social metaphysics is "analogous to the way 'metaphysics' *simpliciter* refers to the deep structure of reality as a whole. So, there are basic existents that constitute the social world, and that should be central to theorizing about it" (Mills, 44). Racial constructivism is the view that race is a social reality. It determines people's social status and hierarchical position but is not an essential property of individuals. This view does what we want our theory of race to do: affirm that we are indeed racially diverse while denying that biological makeup dictates culture, intelligence, or individual abilities.

Racial constructivists are non-essentialists. They believe that one's physical traits (or perceived race) do not reliably predict one's character, abilities, or intelligence. Non-essentialists recognize the power of history, socialization, and environment on one's attitude or culture. Living in an environment that constantly degrades us, or those who belong to our race, will have an adverse effect on how we understand ourselves in relation to others in our society. We internalize the expectation of inferiority and may start behaving as though we were inferior. We might even unconsciously do this to make sense of our negative life experiences. The non-essentialist would say that if a group is generally less advanced in a given society, it does not follow that they are unintelligent, lazy, or unmotivated. Instead, they are less advanced because they have experienced discrimination, perhaps including systemic racism, or because they have been significantly affected by generational trauma. Growing up in a society in which our identity is not valued, we see ourselves differently than we would if raised in a society in which we were considered equal citizens with equal worth and dignity.

Essentialism cannot account for differences among cultures, be they in the United States or elsewhere. If essentialism were correct, all people who are "racially" Iranian should share similar characteristics, including Iranian Americans as well as those living in Iran and other places. Yet, like all identity groups, we hold diverse beliefs and ideologies. Of course, one might point out that "Iranian" designates not a race but rather a nationality or ethnicity, but nationality functions often as a *proxy for race*. "Iranian" like "Mexican" connotes a particular race. Recall the job application that listed two choices for Mexican applicants' race: "Mexican White" and "Mexican Black." We use the term "Mexican" to refer to a particular race and ethnicity. In the United States, the term "Mexican" is commonly used as a racial designation, even though people from Mexico are not "racially" homogeneous. Mexican citizens and Mexican Americans may have European, African, Native, or mixed ancestry. Likewise, "Iranian" as a racial designation refers not to a person's genetic ancestry but to their citizenship or geographical origin.

Although Iranian Americans have been mostly left out of the race dialogue in the United States, our racial designation as "Iranians" refers either to our nationality, Iranian, or the geographic area of the world that we come from, Iran or the Middle East. In her discussion of Asian Americans, Yen Le Espiritu (2017) remarkably comments that Asians in the United States are "deemed immigrants and immigrants are rarely discussed in terms of race" (102). Her analysis resonates with me in discussing both Mexican Americans and Iranian Americans. Asia is a continent and Asian would mean those who have their roots in Asia, but the term "Asian" is not used as nationality but rather as a racial designation. I, incorrectly, marked the "Asian" box for quite some time given Iran is in the continent Asia, before a friend noticed and explained to me that the term "Asian" does not apply to me.

Given the fluid concept of race, someone who is racialized as white in Iran might not be so in the United States. In Iran, anyone who has light skin, light-colored eyes, and light brown hair is considered white. However, in the United States, that individual might not be categorized as white. The "Iranian white" will be more privileged in Iran but may find herself disadvantaged in comparison to "American whites" in the United States. Our definition of race must have the flexibility to account for these differences.

Theories of Race

Minorities are often victims of racial violence due to the way they look rather than their racial categorization. For instance, the Sikh population who is continually attacked in the wake of World Trade Center bombings on September 11, 2001, being mistaken for Muslim (Basu 2016) and the Indian men who were shot in Kansas in 2017, being mistaken for being Iranians. All were attacked because they looked Middle Eastern or Muslim, or they resembled "al Qaeda" members (Pereira 2007). Our theory of race also must help us distinguish among the races. Haslanger's definition of race meets both of the required criteria: It is flexible enough to account for societal differences in the meaning of racial designations, yet it can distinguish among races and racial designations. Moreover, Haslanger's definition of race entails Jorge Gracia's theory of race and challenges Mills's theory—more on this later in this chapter. Consider Haslanger's definition;

> A group is racialized if its members are socially positioned as subordinate or privileged along some dimension (economic, political, legal, social, etc.), and the group is "marked" as a target for this treatment by observed or imagined bodily features presumed to be evidence of ancestral links to a certain geographical region. (Haslanger 2000, 44)

This view leads to a seeming contradiction. If a member of the subordinated racial group "passes" as white (or as a member of the society's dominant race), and they are not victimized by oppression, they are by definition *not* a member of the subordinated race. This is problematic and might violate "the passing constraint" (Mallon 2004, 648): "*The Passing Constraint*: On a constructionist theory of race, passing should be possible and explicable." Consider Adrian Piper's (1992) account of her experience as a white-passing African American woman. Her identity as "really" African American has been challenged because she does not suffer the injustices that darker African American people do. She refers to this as "the suffering test" (Piper 1992). She denies that this test is useful because, in her view, she is connected to other African Americans through their common experiences, not their common suffering.

I propose an "oppression/advantage test" that differs from the suffering test. According to the oppression/advantage test, if Piper's actual identity were revealed (that is, if she failed to "pass"), she would experience oppression like other African Americans. The "oppression/advantage test" is different from the "suffering test" in that, if Piper's actual identity were revealed (i.e., if she failed to "pass"), she would experience oppression like other African Americans. The essential difference is that the oppression/advantage test is based on group experience, whereas the suffering test is individual. This reflects the idea that, some who might not suffer race-based disadvantages are still part of the racial group. Further, I agree with Mills (1998, 51) that "the appearance of R-ness [race-ness] is neither sufficient nor necessary for actual R-ness—though it will generally be a good evidential indicator—for some people may be able to 'pass'" such as my white-passing daughter and the Black people who passed as "white" in the 1930s and 1940s.

It is important to note that although "passing" is not reducible to the "one drop rule", the phenomenon of "passing" rests on ideas about racial "purity"—specifically, the belief that any amount of "Black blood," no matter how minute, makes a person Black, but only "100% white blood," whatever that means, makes a person white. In a white person's line of ancestry, if there is one single Black individual, they are considered Black. However, it does not go the other way. If in the line of ancestry of a Black person, there is a single white person, it does not classify them as "white." This makes it possible for a Black person to "pass"—to "look white" and, crucially, to *deceive others* about being Black. It seems reasonable to assume that the level of animosity towards African Americans made it impossible for white lawmakers to consider anyone with any Black ancestors to be white. But the situation is different for non-Black racial minorities in the United States. For instance, when my daughter challenged her racial categorization at school, the administrators told her that they didn't know how to answer the race question for her and she should just check "white." A child with one Black parent and one white parent, however, will likely be told to choose "Black" or "African American." In other words, the rules do not apply to all people of color in America in the same way, including our rules regarding racial categorizations.

Race is not understood the same way in the Iranian American community. I am a first-generation Iranian immigrant who is not very light-skinned. I speak Persian, and so does my daughter (mostly). And because her father has not been in her life for nearly a decade, all of the people that she identifies as family are Iranians or Iranian Americans. Additionally, we participate in the activities and celebrations of the Iranian American community. Still, some members of my extended family and friends classify her as "white" not recognizing the half of her race she shares with me. This is typical of the experiences of many biracial people. Sometimes they are categorized one way or another. At other times, both of their races are denied by all the groups with which they identify. Additionally, their identities typically are not acknowledged in legal documents. When an Iranian relative met my then two-year-old daughter for the first time, the relative told me that my daughter was "good" because she was American (more specifically, white), not like "rowdy" Iranian children. That is exactly what "internalization of expectation of inferiority" looks like (Bartky 1990). To make matters more confusing, Iranian people generally identify as white and not as people of color. The U.S. Census also classifies us as white ("Census Glossary"). If the relative who called my daughter "good" believes that we are white, that my child is white because I am white, and that the white race is "superior," wouldn't her logic dictate that Iranian children are just as well-behaved as other white children? Is there a difference between "Iranian white" and "American white?" Or do the different shades of "white" truly determine children's behavior? The answers to these questions are wrapped up in our social understanding of the community that we identify with and our knowledge of the negative stereotypes about us and our racial, ethnic, and national identities.

Gracia's (2005; 2017) view on race is especially intriguing: it postulates that those who identify with a racial group but do not share the "general appearance" of people in the group do not actually belong to that race. He argues that our genetic connection to a group of people (ancestry) *and* the physical appearance generally identified with a race together cause us to belong to that particular race. Mills (1998, 50) considers a variety of criteria that can be used to decide one's race: bodily appearance, ancestry, self-awareness of ancestry, public awareness of ancestry, culture, experience, and subjective identification. For Mills, these criteria are not mutually exclusive and are used individually, socially, and politically to racialize individuals and groups. It is commonly thought that ancestry is sufficient to determine a person's race. That is, if one's ancestors are from Asia, then that person's race is Asian. The same thing I said about Mexicans can be said about Asians. The term "Asian" refers to an individual who was born in the continent Asia; however, it is used as a racial designation and applies only to a particular group of people who are born in the continent. By definition, then, people from Iran are also Asians because we are born on that continent. However, the term "Asian" is no longer used that way. Instead, "Asian" typically refers to specific physical traits not shared by Iranians. Furthermore, a minority of white Iranians are indistinguishable from white Europeans. If race were determined by physical appearance, such people would not be Iranians (in America) because their appearance is not generally identified with that race. Moreover, they are unlikely to experience discrimination in the same ways that a darker person of color might.

Because many people around the world have similarities in appearance, our racial categorizations do not always match up with people's identities. An interview with an albino American Black man reveals the identity struggles that he goes through in everyday life (Vernado 2018). He has all the stereotypical physical features of Africans, but he has blond hair and very white skin. He grew up identifying as neither white nor Black. He finds himself at a crossroad of identities that neither community accepts as theirs. When he was in school, both the white and the Black children ridiculed him because of his appearance. Our theory of race must account for the struggles of this individual and "allow" him a race.

Next, we turn to experiential and identification theories of race; "On an *experiential* account of race, anyone who escapes *actually being* classified as a member of race R (and thereby escapes the common experiences of R's) is not an R" (Mallon 2004, 650). On an identification account of race, "one's race is determined simply by what one believes and how one acts" (Mallon 2004, 649). Experiential or identification theories of race require us to label or classify groups. In the case of the former one's experiencing life as a person who has the race R, makes that person belong to that racial group, and in the case of the latter, one's personal and cultural identity, beliefs and practices determines one's race. But these classifications do not fulfill what we expect of a theory of race (Mallon 2004; Michaels 1992, 1994). According to these theories, the criterion for membership in a particular racial group is one's identifying with that group or culture, so these theories cannot account for passing. The notion of passing here makes no sense because, as Walter Michaels (1994, 768) puts it, "to believe and practice what the members of any race believe and practice, by definition make you a member of that race" (Mallon 2004, 650). This view challenges Haslanger's theory of race, because her theory entails the experience of suffering disadvantages due to one's racial classification.

I suggest an amendment to Haslanger's view in order to capture both the non-traveling constraint as well as the passing constraint. The latter refers to the idea that in the constructionist view of race, "race does not ravel" (Mallon 2004, 656), with Michael Root clarifying that "Some men who are black in New Orleans now would have been octoroons there some years ago or would be white in Brazil today" (2000, 631–632). Additionally, in the constructivist theory of race "passing should be possible and explicable" which Mallon refers to as the "passing constraints" (684).

In amending Haslanger's view, I borrow from Mallon (2004), who argues that we need a theory of race that captures ordinary people's view of race, which he calls the *folk theory*. In this new view of race, which is Haslanger's amended theory, the concept of race requires that a community agree on the attributions of a particular race (652).

A group is racialized if

1. Individuals in the group are socially positioned as subordinate or privileged along some dimension (economic, political, legal, social, etc.), because
2. The group satisfies "the criteria central to the application of a folk racial concept" (Mallon, 661) and
3. The individuals within the group occupy a location (a society, culture, or group) within which race is used to divide people.

These criteria are neither necessary nor sufficient unless the group decides that they are. This theory is "objective" in the same sense that Mills's theory is. That is, there are certain criteria by which we (as ordinary people) decide on the extensions of the concept "race." Let's call Haslanger's amended theory the *objectively constructed folk theory*.

OBJECTIVELY CONSTRUCTED FOLK THEORY

In this view, the concept of race is defined by ordinary people. This concept is fluid, does not travel, and accounts for passing. It amounts to the view of race that Kwame Anthony Appiah (1994, 57–58) calls, "vague criterial theory," which conceives race as "something that satisfies a good number of criterial beliefs" but not necessarily all of them. People and groups will vary on their understanding of race depending on which of the criterial beliefs they hold. Criterial beliefs about race are the shared beliefs about the word "race." When we learn about race, we also learn a set of rules that apply to the usage of the categories. This is analogous to the way that we learn about language (Taylor 2013). Language is closely connected to what we know and how we know it. We learn about race the same way that we learn the language, which is spoken by people around us everyday. There are some things that we are taught when we learn the language but most of it, we pick up just from our surroundings. That's the same way that we learn about race and racism.

Linda Alcoff (1996, 8), building on Wittgenstein's concept of language, adds that the "meaning of race will shift as one moves through the terrain and interplay of different discourses, where here discourses signify practices and institutions as well as systems of knowledge." Race is the application of a set of rules we subconsciously or consciously learn, depending on our location, culture, and the way we interpret, use, and understand language. Those rules of language, including the ones about usage of the word "race" and the categorization of racial groups, might vary, but we (those of us who live in a society) share some common understandings. This account is local to a particular place and time, and it can account for passing.

> It is because ascription of racial identities—the process of applying the label to people, including ourselves—is based on more than intentional identification that there can be a gap between what people ascriptively are and the racial identity they perform: it is this gap that makes passing possible. (Appiah 1994, 107)

The theory of race proposed here is not an ontological theory but rather a working theory. Someone who is racialized to be white in Iran might not be so in the United States—hence the constructionist commitment to the no traveling constraint (Mallon 2004). Since I am committed to the constructivist view on race, I also hold to the no traveling constraint.

IRANIAN AMERICAN RACIALIZATION

It is challenging to talk about the racial categorization of Iranians using *objectively constructed folk theory*. According to this theory, for a person to be racialized as belonging to a particular race, they must meet the following criteria.

(1) Individuals are socially positioned as subordinate or privileged along some dimension (economic, political, legal, social, etc.). The negative stereotypes about Middle Easterners, Iranians, and Muslims, as well as the United States' political relations with Iran, are the cause of the discrimination that the Iranian American community experiences. Due to such discrimination,

Iranian Americans experience difficulty finding gainful employment, integrating into their (non-Iranian) communities, and becoming politically active, among other challenges. They are also subject to racial profiling by the police and other authorities. But unlike other minoritized groups, Iranian Americans typically do not suffer from economic deprivation. The community consists of mostly middle- and upper-income families. Studying the Iranian community outside Iran, Mohsen Mobasher (2018) found that

> despite their advanced degrees, professional skills, middle-class or upper middle-class origin, and proficiency in the host country's language, the majority of Iranians in the countries considered in this book [*The Iranian Diaspora*] face relatively similar sociopolitical barriers for integration and suffer from the same identity crisis, such as concealing their ethnonational or religious identity or inventing a new identity as "Persian" that deemphasizes Islamic heritage. (222)

The countries that Mobasher and colleagues considered are the United States, Germany, Netherlands, Great Britain, the United Arab Emirates (UAE), Australia, France, and Italy. The only Iranian community that did not fit the description above was in the UAE. With its prospering economy and geographical location neighboring Iran, it attracts low-wage earners from Iran, where the economy continues to decline and the unemployment rate is relatively high. In the Unites States, Iranian Americans thrive economically, although we are socially and politically marginalized.

(2) Phenotypically, culturally, and ancestrally, most of us satisfy "the criteria central to the application of a folk racial concept" (Mallon 2004, 661). That is, ordinary people racialize us by the way we look and our connection to an ancestral past. We are also racialized through our language, accent, food, holiday celebrations, and other elements of our identity. Most Iranian Americans cannot pass as white, so we are already perceived as "not American." Sometimes our identities seem uncertain or unclear to people. Many of us have been asked about our identity in a somewhat degrading way: "What are you?" as though we are some sort of unusual creature from the world of fairytales.

(3) Iranian American individuals occupy a location (society, culture, or group) within which race is used to divide people. This division is especially confusing for the Iranian American community, because "Iranian American" refers to dual citizenship, or membership in two different national cultures, and not really race. Many Iranians in America identify themselves as Persian to avoid the mainly negative connotations that many Americans associate with Iran, Islam, and the Islamic Republic.

People from Iran have a diversity of physical appearances and racial and ethnic identities due to Iran's geographic location within trade routes, which led to intermarriage of Persians with people from other parts of Asia as well as from Europe and Africa. The U.S. Census Bureau categorizes Iranian Americans, and all people from the Middle East, as white. The racial categorizations in the United States do not include "Brown." Whites and Blacks have racial designations, but other than those, we have the categories Hispanic or Latino, Asian or Pacific Islander, and Native American or Alaskan Native. The Middle Eastern community in general, and the Iranian American community specifically, are completely left out of the population. This is significant because it erases our identity, struggles, and challenges, as well as our contributions to society. Hate groups often target people of color based on their appearance, and our lack of racial categorization therefore leaves us vulnerable to hate crimes without accountability. We are categorized as "white," and hate crime laws do not address "white on white" crime. So, it is difficult to legally argue that any crimes against our community are motivated by racial or ethnic hatred. Moreover, many Iranian Americans likewise categorize their community as "white." This makes it very easy for the justice system to avoid prosecuting racially motivated crimes against Iranian Americans as hate crimes. Mobasher (2012) addresses some of these cases in his book *Iranians in Texas*. Ironically, during the hostage crisis of the 1970s, the Iranian Students at New Mexico State University were protected against expulsion by the desegregation laws passed during the Civil Rights movements, recognizing our "non-whiteness" (Mahdavi 2006).

It is best if our discourse about race is not limited to the realm of politics. To do so would be disempowering, because it allows an outside entity, the political system, to decide on one's identity. Moreover, looking at race as merely "the products of political agendas used to advance the interests of certain groups . . . is dangerous in that it necessarily makes our approach to these phenomena [race, ethnicity, and nationality] political and ultimately a matter of power" (Gracia 2005, 144). If race is merely political, then only the few that have power will define race, and they will do so in a way that benefits themselves. This will leave us "without recourse" (Gracia, 144, 145). Using *objectively constructed folk theory*, on the other hand, is a cohesive way to define race: It considers the political aspect of a race, but also a group's place in the social hierarchy, the group's experience of privilege or disadvantage in the society, the physical appearance that is generally identified with the group, and the definitions of race created by people in the community, which typically incorporates one's appearance and connection to an ancestral past.

As our racial categorizations currently play out socially, we categorize people by their past, their appearance, and their ancestry. We sometimes mistakenly conflate race and ethnicity, and this is sometimes because a person's racial categorization does not fit their ethnic identity. Tommie Shelby points out that such a person "might simply conceal her black [or Persian] ancestry

—as those who 'pass' do—but in either case, she would still be black [or Persian American] . . . even if never found out" (Shelby 2002, 240). Jessica Vasquez refers to this phenomenon not as passing, but rather as "flexible ethnicity," or having the ability to be an insider in two different racialized groups (2010, 46).

Our traditional understanding of race, which is typically based on biological traits and phenotypical differences, is flawed. Race is a combination of personal, social, and politically constructed concepts. A person of color who is white-passing may or may not be racialized as white, regardless of their own personal identity. We might argue that if a white-passing person can live and conduct their lives as a white person with all the privileges that come with whiteness, then they are white, because their non-white identity is no longer economically or politically relevant, and hence ceases to exist.

If we were committed to the idea that race is a socially constructed concept, this is a logical consequent. However, based on the way that race works in our society, this construction is also dependent upon how race is defined by people in society (our second criterion of race). White-passing people of color who are racialized as white, and identify as white, might or might not be racially categorized as white. Those who have multiple racial categorizations sometimes find themselves choosing one of their identities over another. So, a white-passing person of color may or may not themselves identify as a person of color. Moreover, if they have white ancestry in their background, it makes sense to say that, if they experience life as white, under our definition of race, they are white. That same person might *ethnically* identify as a person of color, but that's an ethnicity, not a race. We are racialized by society, but we can choose our ethnicity.

ETHNICITY

Ethnicity is related to race to some extent, but there is no necessary connection between race and ethnicity. Members of a race might not even share history or cultures. For instance, the term "Black" refers to those living in the United States whose ancestors were brought here as slaves, but it also refers to Africans who have willingly moved to the United States, Africans who are currently living in Africa, Iranian Africans who were brought to Iran during the transatlantic slave trade, and even dark-skinned people of India, Mexico, Egypt, and so on. Such people share a phenotype of being dark-skinned, are categorized as "Black," and suffer the similar social disadvantages, yet they all have different ethnicities. Ethnic groups, as Susana Nuccetelli (2004, 254) describes them, "share a complex property supervenient on the history of relations within their group, with others and environment." Ethnic group terms often refer to such groups, and the term could get a referent in many different ways. Consider the ethnic group term "Eskimo," which means "eaters of raw meat" (Nuccetelli, 529). The term was used by the Algonkian tribe to refer to a neighboring tribe who engaged in a cultural practice that they condemned (eating raw meat). The people described by the term "Eskimo" did not use this word to refer to themselves. However, regardless of whether Eskimos eat raw meat or ever did, the referent of the term "Eskimo" is set by pragmatic usage by the Algonkians.

The concept of ethnicity is much broader than race. People of a particular ethnicity are bound historically and culturally more than genetically (Gracia, 148). This distinction is important in understanding one's identity. The *objectively constructed folk theory* of race is not an ontological theory of race but rather a working theory. A race is a group of people who are either advantaged or disadvantaged because they share a (more or less) similar physical appearance typically associated with a particular geographical area. Recall the Asian Indian man who was shot and killed in Kansas because he was presumed to be Iranian. His physical appearance was similar to that of many Middle Eastern people (in this case, Iranians), so he was racialized as such and, for all intents and purposes on that particular occasion, he *was* Iranian. He suffered the same disadvantages in society and was therefore put in the same category as Iranians. Whether he identified as Iranian is not relevant to our concept of race, as long as some people in the community categorize him as Iranian. The race that he was assigned by his murderer might not be the one that he identified with. This might sound absurd; I just wrote that the Indian man who was killed in Kansas is racially Iranian, even though India and Iran are two different countries and not racial designations. However, these terms are used socially as racial designations rather than nationalities. These terms can also sometimes act as *proxies* to ethnicity.

This theory may appear to be overly complex. If the ideas of race, ethnicity, and nationality are so convoluted, what could we possibly mean when we claim to identify with a particular racial group? To start to address this question, let's consider the formation of alliances among different marginalized groups. As marginalized groups make allies of people with whom they share some common identity in order to address their challenges, create change, and fight against their marginalization, a sense of racial identity forms. Essentialism creates in-groups and out-groups, which seems antithetical to the idea of "stronger together" in creating change and making allies. Some who share some common ancestry with people of the in-group might still be considered part of the out-group. Consider Piper's (1992) experience of being a white-passing African American woman who is often told she is not "really Black" because her light skin color gives her white privilege. Is she not allowed to identify as a Black woman because she can pass? To answer this question, I find it important that we discuss the distinction between race and ethnicity and address these sorts of confusions.

In the next two sections, I will discuss the distinction between racial and ethnic identities and respond to concerns regarding racial identity and racial essentialism.

RACIAL/ETHNIC IDENTITY AND THE IRANIAN AMERICAN EXPERIENCE

When we talk about racial identity, we could mean one of two things. First, racial identity with a group of people might mean sharing the same ethnic background. That is, we and our ancestors might share some culture or history with this group of people. This is a case of ethnic identity. The people in an ethnic group might be diverse in their appearance and ancestral backgrounds. Second, we might racially identify with a group based on how we have been racialized and how we have been benefited or disadvantaged because of that racialization. Racialization is dependent upon time and place. For instance, Italian Americans are now racialized exclusively as white, but in the nineteenth century in the United States, they were racialized as non-white.

Writing about Iranians who emigrated to various countries during the 1970s and 1980s, Iranian American anthropologist Mohsen Mobasher (2012, 9) finds that "Iranian identity has become a contested and problematic issue for many Iranian immigrants. The Iranian community in exile suffers from an identity crisis. It lacks a unified sense of national identity strong enough to bind Iranians together." The Islamic revolution created a great divide in Iran, which was reflected in the mutual hostility between Iranians who supported the revolution and those who did not. Due to the grave human rights violations committed by the Islamic Republic of Iran, any display of commitment to Islam by Iranian Americans, creates further division, hostility, and mistrust in the Iranian American community. Ironically, even some Muslim-identifying Iranians left Iran after the 1970s for a better life in the United States. These Iranians face hostility not only from their host country but also from their fellow Iranian Americans. But they are not the only group that feels alienated. The second and third generations of Iranians born in the United States are further alienated from the Iranian American community because their racial and ethnic identities are challenged by first-generation Iranian Americans. Identity policing can occur along multiple dimensions: whether one speaks Farsi (Persian), whether one's children speak Farsi, whether one has a non-Iranian parent, whether one attends the annual Iranian celebrations, and whether one associates with other members of the Iranian American community. These in-group vs. out-group classifications are not only counterproductive and essentialist but, in my view, are also immoral.

We have been forced by circumstances to immigrate to another country and break our families apart. We have lost our homeland, escaped wars, worked hard, tried to assimilate, and hoped for a better future for ourselves and children. For all that, we have found ourselves standing with the Iran hostage crisis always in the backdrop of our lives in America. As described in chapter 1, Iranian American identity is confounded in the space between *Not Without My Daughter, Argo* and *Shahs of Sunset*. If one is male and looks Middle Eastern, those around him may find it difficult to know where in this continuum he stands. It is in this space that we struggle to humanize ourselves in others' eyes and protect our children from the stereotypes that haunt us. It is in this space that we hope we can come together and fight against oppression. But in order for us to come together, we require trust and a common ground. Racial identity brings communities together to fight against their oppression, yet the concept of both race and ethnicity is very much disputed within the Iranian community.

Immigrants and, to some extent, their children stand on the bridge that connects one culture to another. The individuals are scattered over all parts of the bridge. Identity policing from within our community detracts from the development of our authentic identities and erases the emotional security that comes with group membership, especially when the group faces hostility. Those of us who escaped our home country were motivated by the prospect of physical, emotional, and economic security.

Whatever our identity might be, all marginalized and disempowered populations want to end their oppression. The concept of race is complicated and changing. People within a race are diverse. They might or might not share a common goal, a language, a culture, or even an ancestry with the racial group that they have been categorized to be. Race is assigned to a group of people because they look, dress, or act a certain way, or because they are from a particular part of the world that generally is associated with their perceived race. Race is a dynamic social phenomenon that changes as the culture changes and as our stereotypes change and our racial designations are pragmatically chosen. Mallon introduces the idea of *identification with,* "which involves taking the descriptions, narratives, and associations linked with a category as grounds for shaping one's project. [In this sense of racial identity] it seems possible to 'identify with' things that one is not and even cannot be" (2017, 396–397). Mallon gives the example of his father who identifies with the fictional ideas of cowboys and ranchers even though he never was one. In this view, if one is racialized in a particular racial group, one can loosely identify with the group identity in fighting oppression. This is not an individualized sense of identity but rather a socially assigned and recognized designation.

Ethnic identity is a product of family, community, and maintenance of the common culture. "[I]t is perfectly possible for a Black and a white American to grow up together in a shared adoptive family—with the same knowledge and values—and still grow into separate racial identities in part because their experience outside the family, in public space, is bound to be racially differentiated." (Appiah 1994, 117–118). Because they are racialized differently in their community, these two people can share an ethnic identity without sharing a racial identity.

In the case of racial oppression, members identify a group based on their own understanding of their racial categories or ethnicity. Groups and individuals both categorize themselves based on their culture, ancestry, or physical appearance. I will discuss these categorizations in some detail below.

Culture

People are generally visual in their categorization of individuals into groups. With people's appearances come many stereotypes. These stereotypes are what we think and believe about others' cultures. For instance, when we see someone who is Iranian, we have certain cultural expectations that we might not have if we see someone who is white. In the United States near the Mexican border, it is very common to see people who are white but do not identify with mainstream white American culture. They consider themselves Mexican in ethnicity and self-identify accordingly. A white student of mine at the University of Texas Pan American campus, who was born near the border and lived in the United States all of his life, has no white friends, speaks fluent Spanish, and self-identifies with Mexicans. He told me, "My people are Mexican people. I feel alienated when I am around whites only." On the other hand, many Mexicans in the Rio Grande valley in South Texas have lived there for more than a generation, are wealthy, and have integrated into the white culture. They are frequently referred to as "white" and often self-identify as white. They and the people around them, both white and Mexican consider wealth and culture to be the criteria of racial identity. Yet they are not necessarily the "white Mexicans" that the job application was referring to. Some members of this group are dark-skinned and not white-passing. They classify themselves as white because of their socioeconomic class. This is parallel to the self-identification of Iranian American people who do not identify as Iranian because they feel themselves culturally incongruent with the Iranian culture—even though the culture is not just Iranian anymore. Those of us who live in the United States have an Iranian American culture that is distinct from an Iranian culture.

Using culture to define racial identity can be problematic in a society that looks at one's appearance and presumed ethnic background to categorize people. If a person's physical appearance does not conform to the race with which they identify, their self-identity is taken as a case of mistaken identity, like that of my daughter, a white-passing person who identifies as a person of color. Further, given my appearance (brown skin, black hair, and dark brown eyes), I would be considered "the other" even if I had been born in the United States, spoke only English, and celebrated only American holidays. Being "the other" comes with a whole set of cultural expectations, regardless of whether I identify with my Iranian culture. The idea of "the other" was introduced by Hegel (1971), which refers to a person in conflict with themselves. It carries connotations of separateness and alienation, notions that are reflected in a question I am often asked: "Where are you from?" The question does not refer to the city or state where I live but rather my ethnic background. On the other hand, my daughter is not asked about her ethnic background (her race). By contrast, an African American student once told me that her grandfather believed she was not "Black enough," which is a good example of identity policing. His concern was that his granddaughter talked, dressed, and acted like "white" people, so he classified her as "not Black" based on his understanding of Black culture in the United States. Yet this student was racialized as a "Black" woman, identified as one, and faced many of the obstacles that Black women face in the United States.

Although culture ethnically binds us to a group, race is how we are socially categorized. Drawing on the common analogy to an Oreo cookie, which is black on the outside but white on the inside, Mills refers to an "Oreo-man," which describes someone who appears of Black and is socially categorized as Black but who thinks and "lives in" white culture, whatever that might mean to them and their community (Mills 1998, 60). Although culture is important for community cohesiveness, it is not used to racialize people. For example, a white European who has adopted a non-white culture is still considered white, although they might not ethnically identify as such. So, culture might not be a good determining factor for one's formulations of racial identity, yet may still be necessary for ethnic identity.

I will address the following two concerns about using culture as the basis for identity. (1) Shelby notes that preservation of culture is not actually *necessary* for the emancipation of a race (2002, 236). That is, to be taken seriously in a society and be granted full dignity and human value, one need not keep one's culture. (2) This is congruent with Appiah's (1994) concern that, since the Holocaust, we have replaced racial essentialism with cultural essentialism.

I will address Shelby's concern first. Shelby is correct in saying that preservation of culture is not necessary for emancipation of a race. However, if a group's race is important for community cohesiveness, then having to give up their culture (or keep it hidden) to be accepted as equal members of society is oppressive. For example, every year, Iranian communities around the world celebrate the first day of spring as the first day of our new year. Around the same time, we also have a community-wide outing (picnic) and a fire-jumping event. If we have to give up these celebrations to be accepted as equal members of our communities, at best we ought to be alarmed, and at worst we are dealing with cultural imperialism, which "'consists in the universalization of one group's experience and culture, and its establishment as the norm' and is given preferential treatment. Cultural imperialism is most obvious in a society like ours that places minority culture in an inferior status to the majority white culture" (Young 1988, 285, footnote 15). Although culture is not necessary to free a race, it might be essential for preservation of ethnicity. I believe that culture plays a significant role in some people's lives, but I do not advocate for cultural practices that are oppressive to the culture's members, such as child marriages, female genital mutilation, or other harmful beliefs and practices that ostensibly preserve cultural identity. In these cases, cultural identity must be sacrificed for the benefit of individuals' wellbeing. On the other hand, if the only way that a group can achieve equality in a diverse society is to give up its culture, then we are right to be alarmed at the prospect of oppression. Martha Nussbaum points out the importance of saving human functioning and dignity:

> And what we are going to say is: there are universal obligations to protect human functioning and its dignity, and that the dignity of women is equal to that of men. If that involves assault on many local traditions [culture], both Western and non-Western, so much the better, because any tradition that denies these things is unjust. (Nussbaum 2000, 30)

This passage by Nussbaum is a starting point for responding to Appiah's claim that cultural identity might not be a good unifying element because, he states, racial essentialism has been replaced with cultural essentialism, which raises concerns about an in-group/out-group dichotomy. I agree with this concern. As an immigrant who lives in two cultures on a daily basis, I have seen my family give up many aspects of our culture and grow into new ones. Cultures are fluid and changing. We have not lost our personal or group identity, and I suspect that our culture will continue to change. Our cultural practices might connect us as a group only because we were born in a particular place, and not because we share a racial designation. Cultures stem from a group dynamic and do not cause one's racialization or form one's racial identity. Further, "the very idea of a coherent structure of beliefs and values and practices depends on a model of culture that does not fit our times, as we can see if we explore, for a moment, the ideal type of a culture where it might seem to be appropriate" (Appiah 2014, 114).

Given the pluralist nature of our society, including generational differences, language differences, and varying immigration status, it is becoming more difficult to unite under the umbrella of uniform culture as the basis for our cultural identification. It leaves people out more often than it brings them together. So, there are merits to the view that identity based on culture might be more divisive than cohesive, unless we agree on some basic tenets of the culture—as we mostly do—and recognize that cultures are fluid and changing.

Ancestry and Physical Appearance

Physical appearance is often associated with one's ancestry as well as one's race. This can be a bit challenging for those whose appearance does not conform to their racial or ethnic identity, because some people are able to pass as another race. The question of passing is highly debated in communities of color, especially when passing is coupled with denying one's family and ancestry in order to gain privileges. One might argue that if someone has Black ancestry but can pass as white, they are "inauthentic" if they hide their ancestry to avoid the disadvantages that come with being racialized as Black. Appiah points out that passing people "may have prudential reasons for concealing the fact of their (partial) African descent, [but] this will be held by many to amount to inauthenticity, especially if they adopt cultural styles associated with 'white' people" (1990, 498). On the other hand, Appiah argues that race is not a biological classification and therefore is not real in the metaphysical sense. So, if race is not real in the metaphysical sense, why would we say that passing makes someone inauthentic? Appiah's answer recalls Haslanger's view on race:

> . . . for those for whom being African-American is an important aspect of their ethical identity, what matters to them is almost always not the unqualified fact of that descent, but rather something that they supposed to go with it: the *experience* of a life as a member of a group of *people who experience themselves as—and are held by others to be—a community in virtue of their mutual recognition—and their recognition by others—as people of a common descent.* (Appiah 1990, 497. Emphasis added.)

An individual's experience and recognition by others are parts of their race and should be parts of their racial or ethnic identity. Their identity is dependent on their descendants, their place of origin, *and* recognition of such by others in the community. A person who is not recognized as being from that community seems not to meet Appiah's criteria for being of a particular race. Appiah appears not only to have a metaphysical theory of what race is, but also he wants to include self-identification and others' recognition in the concept of a race.

Appiah mixes together two different issues: race and authenticity. According to Appiah, part of being an authentic person is having your race be known to the public. At the same time, part of what it means to belong to a race is the community's identification of you as a member of that race. This appears to generate a contradiction. I cannot be inauthentic about my race if my community does not recognize me as being a member of that race. If we recall the notion that any amount of "Black blood," no matter how miniscule, makes a person Black, it becomes clear that Appiah's view has some contradictions to be sorted out. However, unlike Haslanger's view, Appiah's view is that white-passing Black people with an adopted white culture are still Black, but they are inauthentic Black people. This view is problematic, unless we are committed to the biological view of race, which has been refuted. Race, although a social reality, is not a metaphysical one. If society does not recognize a person to be of a particular race, and race is not a category that biologists use, then that individual is not of that race (Appiah, 498). Both Haslanger and Appiah agree that race is a changing concept, although Appiah is not explicit about it. They agree that some races are racialized in society at some times but not at others. Appiah gives the example of Irish Americans, who were racialized in the nineteenth century and the early twentieth century but are not now; they are not inauthentic if they avoid revealing or acknowledging their ancestry. The theory of race that I proposed earlier, *objectively constructed folk theory*, responds to the worries of passing people. According to this view, those who pass might identify differently from how they are racialized. However, their racial categories are what the ordinary people consider them to be. So, their passing status will not violate their sense of integrity, nor would it compromise their sense of authenticity.

However, another concern about the issues of identity is the worry of falling into the traps of essentialism. I will discuss this in the next section.

RACIAL SELF-IDENTITY AND ESSENTIALISM

The main concern about in-grouping and out-grouping people based on race and ethnicity is that, when we do so, we essentialize who is and who is not allowed to belong. We do the same when we identify with a group of people:

We risk having our racial or ethnic identity fall into essentialism. Stephen Jay Gould (1981, 323) reminds us that

> Although frequencies for difference states of gene differ among races, we have found no "race genes"—that is, states fixed in certain races and absent from all others. Lewontin (1972) studied variation in seventeen genes coded for differences in blood and found that only 6.3 percent of the variations can be attributed to racial membership. Fully 85.4 percent of the variation occurred within local populations (the remaining 8.3 percent records differences among local populations within a race).

Given such vast differences, it makes little sense to group people based on race and to identify with a race. Still, we want to identify with *our* people, whether to maintain a sense of community or to make a political statement in the fight against oppression. But what it is about these people that makes them *our* people? Given that there are few genetic components of our identification with other people, how then do we decide which factors matter in our identification with others, and how do we avoid falling into essentialism? There is no *essential* characteristic—cultural, political, geographical, or other—that binds people together. This is especially true for a community of immigrants with diverse ethnicities, religions, languages, and cultures. Yet in this space of uncertainty, my connection to my community (the Iranian American community) is often the place where I find comfort and belonging. In this community, I know the rules of the game, and I know how to navigate the space, even though there are many different ways of being Iranian American in the continuum of our cultural identity. Our immigration stories, along with the duration of time that we have resided in the United States, have changed our culture from Iranian to Iranian American. Despite this change, however, we know the basic rules, and this knowledge creates a sense of comfort and belonging. There is not necessarily any one way of being that drives us to identify with one another. Our identification is cultural, social, political, and personal.

Michael C. LaBossiere (1997) argues that it is not racial identification that should unite us. Instead, we should identify with one another under the *label* that we are categorized under, and not necessarily with a particular racial group with whom we share some similarity, whether or not we *identify* with members of that group. This way of looking at self-identity becomes more of a political classification than an essentialist categorization of a race. Suppose that I, as an Iranian woman, have been labeled "Hispanic" and suffer the same kinds of disadvantages as Hispanic women, which is what actually occurred when I lived in South Texas. According to LaBossiere, if I am committed to fighting oppression, I ought to unite with other Hispanics, even if I do not self-identify as Hispanic. The term "Hispanic," which the U.S. Census Bureau adopted in 1980, generally refers to people from Mexico, Central America, and South America.

Some people labeled "Hispanic" do not like this term, but their disagreement with the label is not of interest for our purposes here. Terms that label ethnic groups can be set in many different ways (Nuccetelli 2004). The theory of race proposed in this chapter will accept that a person can be labeled "white" in some situations and not others, depending on the context in which they are racialized.

Both LaBossiere and Shelby agree that oppressed people (in their writings, Blacks) should identify with each other based on their common oppression or, in other words, based on the label they have been given and their victimization by virtue of those labels. Whether or not the oppressed person agrees with their label is a different issue that need not be addressed in fighting oppression. That is, we ought not get bogged down in debates about what is a *real* Black, Mexican, or Persian; instead, we should unite in our oppression to fight it. According to Shelby (2002, 254),

> I would urge blacks to identify with each other on the basis of their common oppression and commitment to resisting it; and, from the standpoint of black solidarity, each should be allowed, without molestation, to interpret "blackness" however she or he sees fit (provided the interpretation does not advocate anything immoral and is consistent with the principles and goals of antiracism).

Shelby rightly argues that, once we find ourselves seeking the criteria for racial identity, we are suddenly trapped in a debate about who belongs to our race and who does not. This phenomenon is evident in Iranian culture, especially among those living in the diaspora. Iranian immigrant culture is unsure how to define itself. Many options are available to us to use in defining ourselves, and most of them will create animosity and in-group/out-group dichotomies that are counter to our goal of unity and inclusivity.

The racialist conception of race is bad for identity. Racialism is the grouping of people by the concept of "'races,' in such a way that the members of these groups [share] certain fundamental, heritable, physical, moral, intellectual, and cultural characteristics with each other that they [do] not share with members of any other race" (Appiah 1994, 80). This is a very narrow way to define people. Shelby goes further, giving several reasons for his claim that arguing about the details of racial identity is bad altogether. "First, black people would inevitably become bogged down, as they often have, by disagreements over what constitutes and who possesses an 'authentic' black identity" (Shelby 2002, 245, 249). Although Shelby is talking about Blacks only, the same concern applies to the Iranian American community. On what religion, culture, lifestyle, or political affiliation should we base our racial identity? In trying to figure out which factors should unite us, we become bogged down and lose sight of our goal. I often hear sentiments about who is a "real" Iranian based on criteria that create only division and exclusion.

Second, if people of a particular race try to identify under a single culture, Shelby warns that "class differences among blacks will complicate any attempt to sustain a common black ethnic or cultural identity" (Shelby 2002, 250). Class is one of the most powerful dividing elements in a capitalist society, often defining one's culture and identification independently of race. I mentioned earlier in this chapter that many Mexicans in South Texas consider themselves white, neither because they are racialized by society as white nor because they are light-skinned, but because they are financially successful and they identify race with class. Within a particular social class, there are various races and ethnicities that do not share a unified identity. Class, then, is another factor that divides rather than unites people of different racial categorizations. Thus, "cultural [or class] identity . . . is not necessary for the success of the emancipatory project," but it could be a dividing force between people of a race (Shelby, 250). It is worth mentioning that Iranian Americans have largely avoided the economic difficulties that affect many other marginalized groups in the United States. Because Iranian Americans have had access to education, self-employment, and other entrepreneurship opportunities, they have been "able to side-step economic competition with other Americans [and] avoid additional hostility that might have surfaced had they been seen as taking jobs from native-born Americans" (Mahdavi 2006, 239). Having the opportunity to be self-employed, many Iranians in American have avoided discrimination that they might have experienced in the workplace.

Strict racial and group identities often cause friction between different genders. Iranian identity is largely defined by men. It bothers me that Iranian men are relatively unconcerned with issues that affect Iranian women, be they in Iran or abroad. This indifference toward women's struggles, common in patriarchal societies, places Iranian American women at the intersection of racial and gender oppression. We are in a tough place in society. If we speak of issues such as domestic violence, sexual assault, or other transgressions committed against us by Iranian American men, we are criticized by the Iranian American community for perpetuating unfavorable stereotypes of Middle Eastern men as bullies and abusers, thereby contributing to their oppressed position. Women therefore are often silenced, and their issues ignored. So it's no surprise that women remain silent to avoid perpetuating stereotypical images of Iranian men.

Additionally, the Americanization process and the development of ethnic identity are different for Iranian women in the United States than for Iranian men. Iranians who immigrated to the United States during the 1970s and 1980s were under the assumption that the Islamic Republic regime would fail and they would be able to return home. However, after more than forty years of ruling by an Islamic government, the situation of women in Iran is generally unfavorable; by law, they have far fewer rights and opportunities than men. Iranian women living in the United States therefore have a different experience from Iranian women in their homeland, and this significantly affects the development of their identity as Iranian Americans. In Iran, men have far fewer limitations to overcome than women, but in the United States, Iranian men have experienced greater discrimination than Iranian women have (Sheth 2017). "While Iranian women are often seen as victims of the Islamic regime, men are viewed suspiciously as perpetrators—terroristic, barbaric, and disloyal.... Women, on the other hand, are more often viewed as fellow victims of a common enemy," namely the Iranian government (Mahdavi 2006, 240–241). Vasquez describes a similar gendered racialization with regard to Mexican Americans. Mexican American men are generally classified as being a threat but the women as exotic or docile (2010, 46). This discrepancy affects the dynamics of both of these groups in the United States and disrupts the creation of a cohesive group identity. It is perhaps axiomatic that all people who suffer racial oppression, regardless of their culture, class, or gender, are interested in ending it. During the hostage crisis of the 1970s, and as a result of it, Iranians in the United States experienced a backlash against them, and the "Japanese American Citizens League was one of only a few groups to speak out against the persecution of Iranians in America" (Mahdavi 2006, 222). This is an example of marginalized groups uniting in our oppression to fight against oppression in general. The uniting force is not racial identity. Race is a fluid and changing concept. It depends upon the motives of categorization as well as the social and political climate. We will be better served to unite under common oppression than racial identity, which includes the privilege and discrimination that we experience.

CHAPTER SUMMARY

The *objectively constructed folk theory* of race includes both one's position of harm or privilege in a society that has a hierarchical view on race and the application of ordinary people's understanding of race. Racial categorizations are socially, politically, legally, and economically constructed. This theory of race defines race for a specific time and place, because racial categories are fluid and changing, and racial categorizations do not necessarily travel from one society or community to another. They are dependent on a community's understanding of race as well as its social and political histories. People do not necessarily identify in the way that society racializes them. A person of color who passes as white might not identify as white. However, their racial designation is socially and politically determined. Moreover, I have argued that our racial identity is actually ethnic identity. Ethnicity is what connects us to our histories, cultures, and communities. Ethnic categories are not imposed on us as racial categories are. Instead, ethnicity is the part of our identity that connects us to our ancestral, historical, and cultural past and present.

My interest in studying race and ethnicity is not only to understand the metaphysics of race, but also to articulate its role in the oppression that racial minorities experience. I am interested in uncovering how to fully understand race and racial oppression, as well as how to overcome racial and ethnic oppression. In the next chapter, I will lay out and discuss a theory of oppression with a focus on racial oppression.

Chapter Three

Voluntary Oppression

A SURVEY OF THEORIES OF OPPRESSION

Oppression traditionally has referred to the loss of one's freedom, liberty, or capabilities due to actions carried out by those in power. But today, theories of oppression include a much broader set of ideas. As the previous chapters discuss regarding the Iranian American community, subtle cases of hostility are more common than are outright acts of violence. The Iranian American community is on average more affluent than many other minority groups, yet are forcefully and violently by law or otherwise, prevented from full participation in social, political, and economic aspects of society. Our theory of oppression should account for such cases.

Oppression can refer to "systematic and structural phenomena that are not necessarily the result of the intentions of a tyrant," (Young 1988, 271) but rather can be found in the everyday minds and actions of each citizen, following the oppressive "scripts" of America (Bonilla-Silva 2013, 131), some of whom may not recognize their own participation in oppression. Patricia Williams (1991, 48) expounds on Iris Young's claim that oppression is perpetuated in minds of "good liberals" who believe in equality among people of all races:

> Race-neutrality in law has become the presumed antidote for race bias in real life. With the entrenchment of the notion of race-neutrality came attacks on the concept of affirmative action and the rise of reverse discrimination suits. Blacks, for so many generations deprived of jobs [based] on the color of our skin, are now told that we ought to find it demeaning to be hired, based on the color of our skin. Such is the silliness of simplistic either-or inversions as remedies to complex problems.

In an ideal world, where race does not and never did have any significance, hiring processes would overlook all claims of race, color, and so forth. However, we don't live in those circumstances. We live in a society where race is hierarchial and some races are granted more power than others. As an example, well-meaning liberals often reinforce the status quo by hiring a Mexican American woman to clean their house or a Mexican American man to mow their lawn. This is problematic because, although well-meaning people in positions of financial privilege might pay their domestic workers well, the status quo is being upheld insofar as Mexican American people are being hired to do the types of work that are seemingly reserved for poor Mexican Americans in the United States. At the very least, this keeps them in a low-prestige position holding jobs that confer little power or prestige. Of course, the oppression of these groups might not even be intentional. On a personal level, we can avoid oppressing domestic workers by paying them well and providing opportunities for education. However, combating oppression at the individual level is not enough. We also need government initiatives to help oppressed people improve their quality of life.

The fact that Mexican Americans are overrepresented in domestic work is certainly an example of classism, and perhaps one of racism as well. It is evident that Mexican American domestic workers do not belong to the privileged group in U.S. society. The privileged group is the group that benefits from the oppression of another. Thus, members of the privileged group are in a position to benefit from the oppression of others. Mexican Americans might generally be willing to do these jobs, but the fact that people of financial privilege hire them to do our chores upholds the status quo. Just as society expects people of financial privilege to hire Mexican Americans as domestic workers, it also expects Mexican Americans to accept jobs as domestic workers. In other words, everyone in this scenario is simply doing "what is expected." As Marilyn Frye reminds us, many "of the restrictions and limitations we live with are more or less internalized and self-monitored, and are part of our adaptations to the requirements and expectations imposed by the needs and tastes and tyrannies of others" (Frye 1983, 14). There is no need for forceful governments, tyrants, or abusive spouses. We do what is expected of us.

At the beginning of the second wave of the feminist movement, many women believed that once laws against discrimination were passed, we would be rid of sexism, racism, classism, and so on. But social justice requires much more than making laws (Pateman 1985). For instance, even if a company has an anti-discrimination policy that prevents job applications submitted by members of minority groups from being dismissed, it is likely that the people overseeing the hiring process hold biases, conscious or otherwise, that affect their decision-making. Furthermore, the fact that there is so little social mobility between classes in our society signifies one of two things: either people have accepted their social standing, or society is set up so that it is extremely difficult for people to make dramatic changes in their lives compared to the lives of their parents. The rich stay rich and the poor stay poor. "The chance in which kids can climb up or down the income ladder has remained pretty stable over the last 20 to 25 years . . . An American born at the bottom has about an 8 percent chance of rising to the top" (Reported by Zarroli 2014, para. 6 and 11).

The upshot is that oppression is much subtler than we once thought. As Jean Harvey puts it, it is "civilized." *Civilized oppression* "involves neither physical violence nor the use of law. Yet these subtle forms are by far the most prevalent in Western industrialized societies" (Harvey 1999, 1). To better understand our society, we need a theoretical framework by which we can recognize all kinds of oppression, including those that are not prima facie categorized as such and those that do not have any one specific oppressor. We might find that most of us participate in the oppression of others or ourselves in ways that are quite harmful to them or us. Harvey's discussion of humor, as well as Beverly Tatum's (1997) observation on ethnic jokes as a tool that oppressors use, is fitting here. Harvey reminds us that having a sense of humor is highly prized as a virtue, although in many contexts, such as situations including a power difference, humor is a way of oppressing the one that the joke is about. Identifying the more nefarious ways that oppression works its way into our lives will help us end the attitudes that cause them.

In building such a framework, we first need to identify the criteria by which oppression can be recognized. In this chapter, I survey the prevalent theories of oppression, mainly those given by Iris Marion Young, T. L. Zutlevics, and Ann Cudd. I will then present my view and explain how it differs from those of the authors named above. I focus particularly on Cudd, as her theory is most similar to mine. According to Cudd and Zutlevics's views, there is a set of criteria shared by cases of oppression. Young, on the other hand, argues that there is no unified theory of oppression. I will show that Young's theory of oppression can be reduced to one unified theory.

Next, I will give a critique of Cudd's view and explain how my proposed theory is a more cohesive (inclusive) theory that allows us to identify more cases of oppression, especially as it applies to race. I will end with an example to illustrate how this theory applies to the case of the Iranian American community.

Iris Young: Five Faces of Oppression

According to Young, there is no single criterion or set of attributes that can describe oppression. She presents five categories (or "faces") of oppression, each of which results from the different circumstances that cause each group to be oppressed. Young argues that, if we were to develop a set of attributes (criteria) that all cases of oppression must have, we would reduce all oppressions to merely one and thereby would lose the important subtleties that characterize and differentiate them. Further, Young argues that reducing oppression to one unified theory would overlook some oppressed groups (Young 1990). Alison Bailey (1998) agrees with Young that oppression is not a "unified phenomenon" because each group experiences it differently.

Young's five categories of oppression are: "exploitation, marginality, powerlessness, cultural imperialism, and violence" (Young 1988, 271). Exploitation is the kind of domination that occurs "through a steady process of transfer of the results of the labor of some people to benefit others" (278). Marxist criticism of capitalism aside, cheap labor is essential in some industries, especially farming and domestic work. Cheap labor means that prices for many food items and other common products are relatively low. But the "cost" of low prices is disproportionately borne by those who provide the cheap labor.

According to Young, most racial oppression is marginalization rather than exploitation. Marginalization occurs when "A whole category of people is expelled from useful participation in social life, potentially then subject to severe material deprivation and even extermination" (1988, 281–282). Marginalization in the Iranian American community has been mainly seen in social isolation and cultural criticism. Iranian Americans experience social isolation and cultural criticism rather than financial deprivation. As mentioned in the last chapter, the Iranian American community is generally well educated and affluent, and the community consists of mostly middle- and upper-income families (Mobasher 2018).

Powerlessness "describes the lives of people who have little or no work autonomy, exercise little creativity or judgment in their work, have no technical expertise or authority, express themselves awkwardly, especially in public or bureaucratic settings, and do not command respect" (Young, 283). Many Iranian immigrants who have not been integrated into American society experience this kind of powerlessness in their daily lives outside of the Iranian American community.

Cultural imperialism "consists in the universalization of [the privileged] group's experience and culture, and its establishment as the norm" (Young, 285). In other words, cultural imperialism gives the privileged group preferential treatment. Cultural imperialism is most obvious in a society like ours because we are one of the most diverse societies with different cultures, that places minority culture in an inferior status to the majority (white) culture.

Last in Young's list is violence, which can be emotional as well as physical. She refers to groups that "suffer the oppression of systematic and legitimate violence. The members of some groups live with the knowledge that they must fear random, unprovoked attacks on their persons or property, which have no motive but to damage, humiliate, or destroy the person" (287).

Although Young (1988, 271) argues against a unified theory of oppression, she claims that "all oppressed people share some unjustified inhibition of their ability to develop and exercise their capacities and express their needs, thoughts, and feelings." Certainly, she is not reducing one oppression to another; instead, she gives us a single criterion that all oppressed groups necessarily share. She does not mean that anyone who is prevented from fully developing their capabilities is oppressed; the criterion is necessary for identifying oppression, but not sufficient.

In addition to this criterion, she lists two more. First, she claims that oppression also "refers to systematic and structural phenomena" (271). This I call the systematicity criterion. Second, she says that oppression refers to "structural phenomena that immobilize or reduce a *group*" (273). Oppression is the systematic inhibition of a *group* "through a vast network of everyday practices, attitudes, assumptions, behaviors, and institutional rules" (275). This notion is reflected in Marilyn Frye's (1983) birdcage analogy, which shows how multiple situations and forces work together to oppress a group. "A single assault—even murder—is not oppressive, for there are many categories of human evil besides that of oppression" (Ander 1985, 114). Oppression involves systematic, intentional, and ongoing harm imposed on a group of people, with or without a group knowingly doing the oppressing. Just as long as each person is doing what they do to keep the status quo, the systematicity criterion is met.

Given this list of criteria for oppression, Young (1988, 276) contradicts herself when she says, "Because different factors, or combinations of factors, constitute the oppression of different groups, making their oppression irreducible, I believe it is not possible to have one essential definition of oppression." However, it seems that the only way to understand her position is to say that oppression will entail, at least, that (1) there exists inhibition of capabilities, (2) this inhibition is systematic, and (3) this inhibition is enforced based on one's group membership. These are to be present in all five of the categories ("faces") of oppression that she identifies. The study of oppression is intended to help us identify different cases of oppression. It does not limit us to only one kind of oppression. Oppression must be distinguished from other kinds of harms because it requires us to use a different method to fight it.

T. L. Zutlevics: Oppression as Lack of Resilient Autonomy

Unlike Young, Zutlevics argues for a unified theory of oppression because "By identifying those underlying features which render a situation oppressive, we are less likely to miss categories of oppression not included in Young's list of five" (2002b, 82). Zutlevics adds that "to be oppressed is to be unjustly denied the opportunity for what [she calls] 'resilient autonomy' [RA, hereafter]" (80). RA means having the security to live according to one's values and desires even if the external circumstances, such as political parties, change (88). Zutlevics adds that being denied RA is a sufficient, rather than a necessary, condition for oppression. Resilience exists if the following two counterfactuals hold: first, "resilient autonomy exists if, and only if... were S to decide to change her life [plans] then she would not be unjustly constrained from doing so. Second, [S has RA if] any change in external circumstances... would not present an unjust impediment to S's living in accordance with her values and desires" (88). In the first case, S changes her values based on her own decision, but in the second, she does not. So, according to Zutlevics, one ought to have the opportunity to live a resiliently autonomous life. She adds, however, that RA can justly be taken away. For instance, by jailing criminals, we take RA away from them, but that is justified (assuming just laws). So, the mere lack of RA does not entail that a person is oppressed (84).

The following example demonstrates this. Person A receives an unjust parking ticket. According to Zutlevics, this does not constitute oppression if it causes no long-term harm or financial burden, it is not a part of an intimidation campaign, the individual is not physically harmed, and it does not alter one's life goals or plans. "Life plans," according to Zutlevics (2002a, 425), refer "merely to what it is that a person *broadly wants to do* in and with his or her life, not some inflexible or unchanging set of goals." This definition, if explored in more detail, could potentially fall into a circularity problem. Zutlevics describes oppression as lack of RA. Having RA means having the ability to change or keep one's life plans as one chooses. But suppose a person's life plan, broadly, is to live a non-oppressed life. If they are prevented from living a non-oppressed life, they do not have RA and are therefore oppressed. In other words, they are oppressed because they are prevented from living a non-oppressed life, which is a circular explanation of oppression.

Consider Zutlevics's example of the parking ticket. In this scenario, the ticket is unjust, but it is an isolated event that does not lead to any other instance of injustice, nor does it cause the person who received it to change their plans: to be oppressed is to suffer serious or pervasive injustice" supposedly resulting from lack of RA, but we are not clear about what constitutes "serious or pervasive injustice" (2002b, 88).

A single act of unjust treatment (e.g., getting an unjust parking ticket or being the victim of a crime) could force one to change one's life plans to the point that they are significantly altered. The harms of getting a parking ticket are psychological but one can be a victim of physical harm as well. An example would be someone who is a victim of sexual assault, or other unprovoked physical violence. Susan Brison (2003) recounts her experience of being violently raped in France and how she changed her life because of it. In such a case, Zutlevics would have to acknowledge that some pervasive injustice is done. The crime victim has not altered her personal goals but is no longer able to live according to her values, and previous life plans. Because unjustly receiving a parking ticket could lead to an unjust violation of RA (and, hence, to oppression." Her theory cannot distinguish between oppression and other kinds of injustice, because it does not make a distinction between *structural or systemic harm* (lack of RA) and harm caused by isolated events. Moreover, her theory does not include a group membership criterion. The crime-victim example does not change the analysis of Zutlevics's case, but it points out that her view does not capture crucial distinctions between oppression and other kinds of injustice. Our theory must identify some particular kind of injustice that counts as oppression. Perhaps Zutlevics would argue that all "serious or pervasive injustices" that unjustly take away RA are oppression. But this introduces the problem of reduction that Young is concerned with, wherein oppression is reduced to refer to any harm. I disagree with this formulation of oppression. I believe that oppression is a particular kind of injustice done on a social level based on a group membership.

Let's examine the claim that oppression is a particular kind of social and/or political injustice. To say that any event that makes a person change their life plans (as lack of RA entails) is oppressive is too broad and doesn't get to the heart of what we want our theory of oppression to do. It is also subjective. Oppression is a kind of harm inflicted on a group. Not every lack of RA is a designator of oppression. We would be defining oppression very broadly if we said that *any* event that makes a person change their life plans (as lack of RA entails) is oppressive. Such a broad definition of oppression is problematic because it may lead us to discount or disregard the significant harms done to the oppressed. I do not believe lack of RA is a sufficient condition for oppression, because there are cases in which RA is violated that are not cases of oppression, even though harm is done. At best, we could conclude that the unjustified denial of RA in some cases points to an oppressive situation. However, we are not sure what those cases are or when RA can be justly taken away.

Furthermore, this definition of oppression cannot account for the more subtle case of psychological oppression. Those who are weighed down with psychological oppression might change their circumstances if the political environment changes, but they might not see it as a threat to their lives as they would if they were not suffering from false consciousness. After the Islamic revolution in Iran in 1979, the propaganda convinced some women to give up their public lives and become confined to their home lives, and second-class status. "Creating panic out of easy to perceive changes in the 'natural' division of labor between the sexes has been a practical strategy for religious and conservative leaders to condemn the existing patterns of change in one society" (Chubin 2014, 45) It was no different in Iran. This is a case of Iranian women changing their lives "willingly" after the "political environment" changed, and claiming they are just doing what is the natural order of things. Before the revolution, these same people held different beliefs even though they could choose differently. Their religion didn't change, nor did the religious beliefs require them to attend only to their home life—namely, there was no coercion involved before the revolution for the women to remain second-class citizens. Cudd makes the distinction between the empirical theory of coercion and the moral theory of coercion. The former claims that a person is coerced only if she feels coerced. The latter suggests that, although she might not feel coerced, she *is* coerced because she is denied some right (Cudd 1994, 26, 31). In the example above, among other things, the women lost the right to hold certain jobs, keep their children after divorce, and not get married until they reached the age of eighteen. Here, we are concerned with the moral theory of coercion, because we want to determine whether a person is coerced, rather than identifying how she feels about her situation. Likewise, we should make distinctions between empirical and moral cases of oppression. Someone who, objectively, is psychologically oppressed, might not consider herself oppressed.

On a final note, even if this broad theory of oppression allows us to distinguish between oppressive and non-oppressive behaviors, it does not give any background reasoning about why RA is so universally important. At best, it merely *correlates with* what makes a situation oppressive, rather than *explaining why* it is oppressive. Many cultures do not consider autonomy valuable, so we must address why having RA is important and why its lack is a sign of oppression. Zutlevics does not answer these kinds of concerns. Although I agree with Zutlevics that there is one theory of oppression, I believe that Cudd's view takes us closer to that theory.

Ann Cudd: Four Criteria for Oppression

Cudd (1994, 25) gives us four necessary and jointly sufficient criteria for oppression. First, "oppression must involve some sort of physical or psychological harm." Harm can be either justified or unjustified. An imprisoned convicted criminal is harmed, but the harm done is justified, so it is not oppressive. Oppression is always a harm, but not all harms are oppression. Oppression is a harm that unjustly limits one's "freedom or choice *relative* to others in one's society." If everyone in a society is harmed in the same way for the same reasons, such harm does not indicate oppression. For instance, consider a country in which no one, including people in government positions, has access to running water. Although lacking running water is a kind of harm, it does not show oppression of any particular people in a society.

Second, harm must be inflicted by people in a more privileged social group upon people in a less privileged social group due to their membership in the less privileged group. Social groups are those that individuals belong to "independently of their oppressed status . . . [one] that they closely identify with, so that the harm attaches to their very self-image," including groups based on race, gender, sexual orientation, and religion (Cudd 1994, 25). I suggest that it is possible for individuals to be socially categorized into groups with which they do not necessarily identify. However, the person who has been categorized in this way can still suffer the harm of oppression due to other factors, which I will discuss in the coming pages.

Third, the social group that is doing the oppressing must benefit from the oppression. This does not mean that every single member of the oppressing group is actively and knowingly an oppressor, but even those who are not active oppressors benefit in some way from their membership in the oppressing group. The benefits of membership in the privileged group are wide-ranging, including elements such as greater respect, better jobs, higher salaries, access to political office, and so forth. Whether they know (or desire) it or not, those in the privileged group who fight for social justice still benefit from the oppression of oppressed groups. Cudd (1994, 25) points out that "typically cases of oppression involve persons who reinforce the status quo social norms without thereby intending to harm anyone else, or even without being aware that upholding the status quo could harm others." That could be those of us in any group, more privileged or less privileged, who continue doing what society expects of us without challenging the system. Susan Stark (2004) takes this idea a step further. She claims that everyone in U.S. society contributes to African Americans' oppression by living and paying taxes in a society in which the government is mainly made up of white upper-class men. This implies that African Americans contribute to their own oppression. This may seem like blaming the victim, but I think she brings up an interesting challenge for a future project.

Fourth, oppression must include some kind of coercion or force. Coercion is a "lack of voluntary choice" (Cudd 1994). Cudd reminds us that we always have a choice, even in coercive situations. For instance, if we are mugged, we have a choice of giving up our wallet or risking our lives. But when we "choose" to give up our wallet, it is not a free choice and, therefore, has a different moral standing than a choice that is free. So, coercion is not "absence of all choice, but a lack of the right kind of choice [voluntary choice]" (Cudd 1994, 27). According to Cudd, coercion is always wrong and is what accounts for the injustice of oppression. For an injustice to count as oppression, the injustice must be forced (or coerced). Cudd adds that, when we judge something (objectively) as coercive, we ought to look at it through a moral lens rather than an empirical one. That is, we must ask, does this situation deny someone a right that they are entitled to? Or does someone merely feel coerced? If we consider the latter case to constitute coercion, we will end up with a subjective account of coercion. As a result, any situation in which one might be faced with a hard decision could be deemed coercive. Cudd agrees with Robert Nozick's account of coercion; coercion "should be judged against a background moral theory that takes autonomy, as well as property rights, seriously" (Cudd, 1994, 31). Her account of coercion is backed with a rights-based moral theory. She later points out that, although this view deals with coercion at the individual level, institutions are capable of coercion as well.

AMENDED CUDD'S THEORY OF OPPRESSION

With four revisions, my theory of oppression closely parallels Cudd's theory. I will discuss my revisions in the following sections.

One: Coercion

I do not believe that coercion is always wrong. Therefore, in my view, coercion cannot stand alone to explain the injustice of oppression. In the ordinary use of "coercion," including Cudd's, a prisoner (let's say a murderer) is coerced: he is actively and intentionally forced to remain in a particular place, perhaps for life, against his will. Although his rights to autonomy and to living a free life have been violated, this violation (coercion) is justified by society's need to prevent future attacks on others. Cudd likewise agrees that some kinds of harm are justified. So, the presence of harm alone is not always a sign of oppression, either. She writes, "to make a claim of oppression is to show that the harms involved are unjustified, or correlatively, to show that some harms are justified is to show that they are not oppressive" (23). In my view, harm is normative, and it is a violation of one's capabilities. For Cudd, coercion is the normative criterion of oppression.

Often, the more subtle kinds of oppression are not coercive. Consider cases of psychological or internalized oppression. For instance, a Black college student might think she lacks an aptitude for math because no one has ever encouraged her to take advanced math courses and the media portrays "math nerds" as white men. Although she would like to be a computer scientist, she chooses to major in psychology instead. No coercion or force is involved; this student made the voluntary choice to forgo a career in computer science, even though other options were available to her. Those are often cases with no coercion or force involved, in which individuals have the choice to make decisions beyond the ones they did make and so there is no *lack of voluntary choice*. The choices are perhaps politically available to them, but they will not make choices other than ones that their society or culture demands of them. Sandra Bartky (1990, 22) defines psychological oppression as follows.

> To be psychologically oppressed is to be weighed down in your mind; it is to have a harsh dominion exercised over your self-esteem. The psychologically oppressed become their own oppressors; they come to exercise harsh dominion over their own self-esteem. Differently put, psychological oppression can be regarded as the "internalization of intimations of inferiority [Cook 1970]."

The psychologically oppressed will not often consider themselves oppressed. They are not coerced or forced to make choices that are harmful, nor are they forced to accept their inferior position. They believe that whatever their social or political status is, they have freely and voluntarily chosen it, although their status is one of inferiority. To use Marx's terms, they suffer from false consciousness. According to Bartky, suffering from false consciousness is to be "Systematically deceived as we are about the nature and origin of our unhappiness, our struggles are directed inward toward the self, or toward other similar selves in whom we may see our deficiencies mirrored, not outward upon those social forces responsible for our predicament" (1990, 31). That is, we are taught that if we are not happy with our lives, the fault is some deficiency that we suffer from rather than the social forces that keep us down. In other words, the victims are blamed for their predicament, sometimes in dismissive ways. They are often told that they are overreacting, oversensitive, or too serious, or that they can't take a joke.

The oppression of a group usually continues by voluntary (non-coercive) acts of the oppressed members of that group when they internalize the social expectations placed upon them. These are cases of developing adaptive preferences (Nussbaum, 2001) or of deformed desires (Cudd, 2006). In these situations, we make the choices that are expected of us or that we are *en-*

couraged to make; "the oppressed are co-opted through their own short-run rational choices to reinforce the long-run oppression of their social group" (Cudd 2006, 22).

Iranian Americans who have faced microaggressions and have seen the typical media representations of themselves (ourselves) will minimize interaction with the non-Iranian community or do the opposite and minimize interaction with the Iranian American community. They are in a double bind. The former strategy reduces our opportunities to integrate into our larger community and to learn how social situations work, thereby curtailing our ability to navigate unknown spaces. Those who minimize their interactions with the non-Iranian community do not experience life as a cohesive continuum of experiences, but rather shift in and out of the unknown place of the non-Iranian community. This limitation is restrictive and even crippling, and it exacerbates the disadvantaged status of those who adopt this strategy. In chapter 1, I discussed the harms associated with leaving one's community and assimilating into the larger community. This is an expected facet of the immigrant experience, as has been reflected in my own immigrant journey. However, I have personally noticed that people who have a more difficult immigrant experience tend to be more likely to deny and even harshly criticize their heritage in order to fit in. The harms perpetuated by this kind of self-hate are mostly psychological, affecting both those who figuratively turn their back on their heritage and those whom they leave behind. This is divisive and hurtful for a community that is already struggling with racism and negative stereotypes.

Those who are not part of the Iranian American community generally notice neither the negative stereotypes and media portrayals of Iranian Americans nor the deleterious effect that these detrimental messages have on the community. Negative stereotypes and negative media portrayals can nevertheless be identified as injustice on the basis of how oppression results from unjust constraints that do not constitute coercion as defined by Cudd (absence of voluntary choice). After all, most Iranian Americans appear to be thriving, and, economically, they might be. The situation is, at least potentially oppressive, though not coercive.

Two: Systematicity Criterion

Another way in which my theory differs from Cudd's is that it includes a systematicity criterion. I assert that, for a group to be oppressed, there must be many interconnected factors involved in suppressing them. This point is implicit in Cudd's group membership criterion, but my theory makes it explicit. Frye's birdcage analogy is an interesting illustration of the systematicity criterion. If we look closely at a birdcage, we do not see it in its entirety.

Instead, we see individual wires, none of which by themselves are capable of confining a bird. But "cageness of the birdcage is a macroscopic phenomenon" (Frye 1983, 7). That is, we must take a broader view of it to see how the many tiny wires work together to imprison the bird. The birdcage is "a network of forces and barriers which are systematically related and which conspire to the immobilization, reduction and molding of [oppressed groups] and the lives [they] live (87). The bird is physically enclosed by the wires, which are analogous to the systematic forces that work together to constitute oppression.

We can discern many forces arranged in a way that perpetuates the inferior status of oppressed groups. Works by Babak Elahi and Persis Karim (2011), two Iranian American scholars writing on the Iranian diaspora, shed light on the systematic forces that constitute this community's oppression. The scholars use the term "diaspora" because the mass emigration of Iranians in the 1970s and 1980s was prompted by the acts of the government. The Iranians who have left Iran in the last forty years have been diverse in religion, ethnicity, age, education, and financial status. Most, but not all, are affluent and highly educated. Some who immigrated decades ago now have children and even grandchildren born in their new country. The forces that limit them vary; most contend with the negative stereotypical images of Iranian people or with cultural barriers, and many also struggle with language or their Muslim status. They worry about their physical and financial security. Refugees, students, and asylum seekers often face economic challenges while lacking community and family support. Iranian Americans started becoming disenfranchised economically and socially during the Iran-Iraq war and the hostage crisis of 1979–1981. Since that time, companies, schools, and other social institutions have overtly excluded Iranian Americans from participation. Iranian Americans' insecurity about engaging with the American community has been passed down to their children, who were born in the United States but surrounded by Iranian American culture in their homes. These children's perceptions of the United States thus differ from those of their parents and grandparents. Today, much of the overt racism towards the people of Iran has faded, but the negative images still haunt the community. These cause systematic physical and emotional harms, some of which I will discuss in chapter 5. Our community looks wealthy, well-adjusted, and well-integrated from the outside, but the internal struggles and limitations are abundant.

Three: Being Cautious

I would like my theory to err on the side of inclusion regarding cases of oppression that we do not yet know about. Therefore, I hold that these criteria are jointly sufficient and not necessary. If x meets my criteria, it is oppression. This gives my theory the flexibility to account for future growth in our ideas of oppression. One way to think about this is to consider Young's theory of the five faces of oppression. Imagine that someone points out a situation that seems to be oppression but is not characterized by the five faces. Would we want to say that this situation cannot be oppressive? I think not. A good theory allows room for new examples of oppression that we might not have thought about yet. Therefore, we should take epistemic caution and avoid establishing necessary criteria for oppression.

Four: Lacking Metaphysical Background

Cudd's theory lacks the required metaphysics to establish oppression as an injustice. This is not a flaw in her view; her work is to be read as a part of a larger dialogue and literature on oppression. The metaphysics I propose uses Martha Nussbaum and Amartya Sen's capabilities approach as a basis for rights in order to provide us with a metaphysics for oppression. The capabilities approach is a theoretical framework for evaluating individual's well-being. The theory is developed significantly by Sen (1984, 1987) and Nussbaum (2000, 2001). Capabilities refer to the things that people are "actually able to do and to be." This metaphysics could apply to all theories of oppression. Therefore, the capabilities approach also explains both why RA is important and why its lack is associated with oppression. According to both Nussbaum and Sen, capabilities are necessary for a flourishing human life. To take away a person's capabilities is both a harm and an injustice. I will say more about the capabilities approach in the next chapter. Before moving on, I will briefly address the concepts of coercion and voluntariness.

COERCION AND VOLUNTARY ACTIONS

The word "coercion" can be used normatively or not. Like harm, coercion is not necessarily unjust. The presence of unjust harm, together with the other criteria of oppression, is sufficient to make a situation oppressive. Most subtle cases of oppression do not involve coercion. Cudd's "Lisa and Larry" case illustrates more subtle examples of oppression.

In her article "Oppression by Choice" and her book *Analyzing Oppression,* Cudd has us consider Lisa and Larry's situation (2006, 148–150). Lisa and Larry are a married couple who both hold jobs outside the house. They decide to have a child and want one parent to stay home to care for her or him. They consider their options and rationally decide that it is financially beneficial for them if Lisa stays home and Larry works. Men are paid more in our society and are more likely to get promotions and pay raises. Therefore, even if Lisa and Larry start out with equal salaries, they likely will not end their careers with equal salaries. For this reason alone, they will probably be in a better financial situation in the future if Lisa stays home. In Cudd's scenario, Lisa and Larry shared household chores when they both worked. After Lisa quits her job, Larry assumes the burden of being the sole financial provider. This causes him stress, and he believes it is his right to do fewer household chores when he gets home from work. Therefore, more of the household chores fall to Lisa, in addition to the childcare duties. Cudd concludes that this situation leaves Lisa at least in a less advantaged situation than Larry, regardless of whether they stay married (Cudd 1994, 37, 38). It is quite easy to think of benefits of working outside the house in a labor market that is valued and paid; Larry benefits from having a higher social status, socializes with people outside the house, has less housework, and spends far less time performing childcare duties. Lisa's labor at home, on the other hand, is not valued in society and, because she leaves the job market, her future labor loses value. So, she has made a rational (according to Cudd, *apparently* rational), voluntary, and informed decision that has left her in an oppressive situation. According to Cudd, Lisa is oppressed because her choice was coerced (not voluntary) because if she had chosen otherwise, her family would not be as well off as they are because her husband works and not her. At first glance, though, she seems to have voluntarily chosen to stay home, and she could have chosen otherwise with no individuals or institutions keeping her from working.

Society is structured in a way that advantages some groups over others. Certainly, Lisa had the option of remaining employed instead of Larry, but the couple had good reason to believe that their family would end up in worse financial shape if Lisa worked rather than Larry. This example can be used to illustrate forms of oppression other than sexism. For instance, consider the case of an interracial (say Black and white) homosexual couple who have a child. As they decide which one should stay home to care for the child, they must consider that the Black partner (be they male or female) will likely make less money than the white partner and therefore should probably be the one to leave paid employment if they are to maintain their quality of life. In a completely egalitarian society, the question of race or gender will not come into play as partners decide who should leave their job to care for children. Even if we agree that there is no coercion involved and everyone acts voluntarily, our society is structured in such a way that rational decision-making leaves us in oppressive situations. Lisa and Larry's situation is an example of this, and Lisa is not alone; due to the choices that people have in our society, "women are coerced in making the choice to eschew economic power and status for domestic servitude.... This implies that women are oppressed by the vicious cycle phenomenon, and thus by means of their own individually rational choices" (Cudd 2006, 151). As an educated person with a supportive spouse, Lisa actually has the tools to carefully consider the situation and understand the options in order to make the best choice, but many others do not.

We can say one of two things about the voluntary status of Lisa's decision. On the one hand, we could assert that Lisa's decision is not voluntary because of the way the society is set up. If she had continued working and Larry had given up his job, the family would likely end up in a worse financial situation. The forces that discriminate against women in the workplace coerce her decision. According to Thomas Mappes (1992, 209–210), "a person can ... be effectively coerced by being threatened with the withholding of something (in some cases, what we would call a 'benefit') to which the person is entitled." In this case, Lisa is coerced into leaving her job because if Larry does so instead, they will not benefit from his probable higher income. So, according to Mappes's definition and Cudd's analysis, Lisa did not choose voluntarily and is therefore oppressed. On the other hand, we could say that Lisa is not coerced and that people can (and sometimes do) make voluntary decisions that leave them in oppressive situations. Cudd makes the former claim, but I will argue for the latter.

Oppression is perpetuated most readily when the oppressed internalize the social expectations of them. By making choices that the oppressors want them to make, they continue their own oppression. The psychologically oppressed often come to believe that their choices were their own authentic choices, freely made. In other words, having been given the illusion of choice, a person may not *feel* coerced and therefore may not believe her decisions were forced.

Coercion

Feeling free from force or coercion is not always a good indication of actual freedom. According to Mappes (1992, 209), one way for us to determine whether our choices are coerced is to ask, "Does the proposal in question have the effect of making a person *worse off upon noncompliance?* ... The person who makes a threat attempts to gain compliance by attaching an undesirable consequence to the alternative of noncompliance. This person attempts to *coerce* consent." The idea here is that if we are trying to avoid a bad consequence by consenting, then our consent is forced and morally questionable. Imagine a person who is told that she will have to either undergo female genital mutilation or face starvation because, in her society, she is not allowed to work if she does not undergo the procedure. She might oppose the practice of female genital mutilation, but she *consents* to undergo it. Despite her consent, this is coercion. She was forced to do something because her refusal would bring about intolerable consequences. A person's decision-making is clearly constrained when their consent is obtained under conditions in which noncompliance results in the withholding of the opportunity to exercise a basic human capability. The circumcised woman loses one capability to preserve another capability; namely, she loses bodily integrity to preserve her life. That is morally alarming. In a just society, we must not be forced on the basis of our identity as a member of a subordinate social group to choose between our bodily integrity and life. However, not every forced choice constitutes oppression. For instance, If I have a life-threatening tumor on my arm, I will likely consent to having my arm cut off to save my life. Although this choice is forced, it is merely an unfortunate medical situation, not an example of oppression, because it is not forced on the basis of my identity as a member of a subordinate social group. In this way, my choice to have my arm cut off differs from the choice of the woman who faces genital mutilation. In summary, according to Cudd, an action is coerced if it is not a voluntary act. Mappes argues that a voluntary act is one that is not backed by any threat. So, both Cudd and Mappes hold that lack of voluntary choice is coercion. Cudd does not define voluntariness, but Mappes does, and his definition entails Cudd's.

Cudd
    ~ Voluntary → Coercion   ~V → C

Mappes
    Threat → Coercion   1. T → C
    ~ Threat → Voluntary   2. ~T → V
                                            3. ~V → T Logically equivalent to 2
                                            4. ~V → C 1, 3 Hypothetical syllogism (Cudd's)
                                            5. ~C → V Logically equivalent to 4

I believe we have to find a way to separate the concepts of voluntariness and coercion. Some situations involve no threat and yet lead to choices that are not voluntary. In other situations, a person may be forced to choose B or C because she is forbidden to choose A. For instance, Maria lives in a country where high schools are single-sex. The Technology School is for boys, so she is forbidden to attend it. However, she can freely choose to attend the Music School or the Liberal Arts School, which are both girls' schools. So, although she is forced to choose one of the girls' schools, she faces no threat for choosing either of them. However, she *is* under threat (be it emotional or physical) if she tries to attend the Technology School. This example shows that to define coercion as a lack of voluntary choice is to define it too broadly. This is because we confront many obstacles that sometimes force us to make decisions contrary to those we wish to make. We do not want to say that any action performed under any shadow of force or coercion is involuntary. Indeed, anyone who lives in a capitalist society, regardless of one's status, is coerced into a choice between working and suffering financially. But we hardly want to argue that all workers in a capitalist society are oppressed. It is true that Lisa is oppressed. It is true that she was faced with a hard choice. However, she made a voluntarily choice, even though larger forces were at work. We thus need a definition of voluntariness that accounts for the case of Lisa and Larry. Let me start with Aristotle's definition of voluntary actions.

Voluntary Actions

According to Aristotle, actions are voluntary if they are not done through some force external to the agent and not done under ignorance: "what is involuntary is what is forced or is caused by ignorance, what is voluntary seems to be what has its origin in the agent himself when he knows the particulars that the action consists in" (1985, 58). "Particulars" refers to the components of decision-making—basically, knowing who is doing what, how, why, and in what way. According to Aristotle, there are six particulars; if we are ignorant of these, our action is involuntary. In his words, the particulars are:

1. who is doing it
2. what he is doing
3. about what or to what he is doing it
4. sometimes, with what he is doing it (e.g., with what instrument)
5. for what result (e.g., safety)
6. in what way (e.g., gently or hard)

Of the six particulars, Aristotle finds (2) and (5) the most important (57–58). Ignorance of these two means that we do not know what we are doing or what the results of our actions will be. We can easily agree with Aristotle's criterion that actions are non-voluntary if performed due to a force external to the agent. But his second criterion of non-voluntariness, ignorance of the six particulars, is questionable.

We are ignorant of many things when we make decisions. Unlike Aristotle, I propose that one can act voluntarily even if one is ignorant of the particulars, although I would add that, if some harm is done, one is not necessarily morally culpable for it. As an example, consider a "mad doctor" who fills a patient's medicine shot with cyanide. The patient dies, of course. The nurse acted voluntarily in giving the shot, but she had no intention of killing the patient and was ignorant of the contents of the shot, so she is not responsible for his death. So, at best, we can say that she did not voluntarily kill the patient. If we take the six particulars seriously, then we must conclude that the nurse's action was involuntary, due to her ignorance of the shot's contents. But this is not the case: She voluntarily took a needle and administered a shot to her patient. That was a voluntary act; killing the patient was not. Aristotle's view cannot account for the subtleties of such cases.

In my view, actions are voluntary if they are undertaken without physical or emotional force. Unlike Aristotle, I do not consider ignorance to count against an action's voluntariness. We often make decisions voluntarily, yet in ignorance of the six particulars. For instance, a first-year college student who chooses history as her major and ends up becoming a successful historian might not know of other majors that might interest her, or the details of pursuing a graduate degree, or what a career in history entails. Many of us were ignorant of such things when we chose our fields of study. Although she is ignorant about her choices, she acted voluntarily. No one physically or mentally forced, coerced, or threatened her to major in history. Although this might not be an informed choice, she is not coerced. Nor was her choice involuntary, nor would there have been any bad consequences had she chosen to study philosophy or math.

Coercion, on the other hand, involves active forces such as social structures, laws, attitudes, lack of social justice, and so forth. This contradicts Aristotle's view of force. He believes actions performed under duress are not forced. My view, on the other hand, is that actions performed under duress sometimes count as forced; it depends on the kind of pressure. Life pressures are certainly a determining factor in our decision-making process. Often, we assume that people are choosing freely to do as they wish, as long as there are no physical forces involved. However, actions can be coerced due to factors other than physical force. For instance, Lisa was forced to choose to give up her job even though no direct forces were involved. According to Cudd (2006, 135), "Direct forces cause inequality through the intentional actions of a dominant group on a subordinate group." All direct forces are socially imposed, and the individual decision-maker is not at all responsible for them. For instance, Lisa's society does not forbid her from working after she becomes a parent, as was the case in the 1930s. On the other hand, there are indirect forces that mold the oppressed in the more subtle ways that Aristotle does not consider. "Indirect forces cause inequality through the choices and decisions of the members of the oppressed group themselves, as they try to live in the face of other inequalities and injustices" (Cudd 2006, 135). In this way, members of oppressed groups internalize society's expectations, such that "the oppressed seem to shape their preferences to embrace the feasible set of options they are faced with" (153). These kinds of forces are not obvious, nor can they be immediately stopped. We are all socialized into our roles, and those roles are the forces that often direct our decision-making. Contra Aristotle, we have to recognize that many instances of force are not obvious. Given this, we can and often do still make voluntary decisions under the shadow of these forces. Perhaps there is a fine line between actions that are involuntary and those that are coerced. Particular actions might be voluntary even while the social, cultural, or family structure is psychologically coercive. This is an example of psychological oppression. Although decisions made under such conditions can be voluntary, we can use Aristotle's criteria to explain how they can still count as coerced.

More on Psychological Oppression

Members of oppressed groups may internalize forms of systematic, institutionalized social and political oppression. By various means, the oppressed internalize political and social expectations and become their own oppressors. As pointed out earlier, Bartky calls this psychological oppression. Psychological oppression encompasses various categories: alienation, sexual objectification, and stereotyping, among others. Alienation occurs when people are separated from basic characteristics that make important contributions to their development as human beings. Objectification occurs when an individual's body parts are distinguished from their personality and treated as though they entirely define—or are the most important features of—their personhood. Stereotypes often portray Iranian men as violent and untrustworthy. Stereotypes are often self-fulfilling, leading stereotyped people to display the attitudes or behaviors expected of them. Those stereotyped to be dangerous or violent internalize that stereotype as a part of themselves, and thereby either adopt violent behaviors as a form of identity or live in fear of being treated as violent. They might internalize this view of themselves and self-identify with the boundaries set for them by society. In my view, a practice is oppressive if it systematically and unjustifiably limits people's development of their capabilities, deprives them of the benefits routinely enjoyed by others, or assigns them to inferior status due to their group membership, by force or otherwise. Oppression is not always obvious; it often requires close analysis and careful observation of a society's treatment of its people. When a group is politically or economically subordinated, often the members of that group internalize the social expectation of them (the oppressor's expectations) and become their own oppressors.

CHAPTER SUMMARY

I agree with Cudd and Zutlevics that there is one theory of oppression. But Zutlevics's theory is too broad and does not give a metaphysics for why she believes that resilient autonomy is important. It does not distinguish between cases such as crime, accidents, or oppression. It is crucial that we do this, because the solutions to each of these cases differ. My theory closely parallels Cudd's. In my view, an act is oppressive if it meets the following criteria: one, there is some kind of harm done, with people's capabilities unjustly taken away. Two, it is perpetrated based on group membership. Three, another group benefits from it. Four, the oppression is systematic. In short, to be oppressed is to have one's capabilities systematically thwarted or taken away (following my definition of harm) because of one's group membership, in order to benefit another group, whether the harm done is voluntary or not. My theory of oppression picks as many cases of oppression as Cudd's. If we can capture all oppressive situations without introducing coercion, we should do so, because coercion introduces a whole new debate. In the next chapter, I discuss the capabilities approach, which I will argue is the basis of rights, and their violation constitutes harm.

Chapter Four

Bridging the Gap Between Rights and Capabilities

THE ROADMAP

In the study of oppression, we can find ourselves falling into the trap of making circular arguments, or begging the question, as Ann Cudd (1994, 2006) does in her theory of oppression, discussed in the previous chapter. As mentioned in the last chapter, this is not a flaw in her view. In this chapter, I provide a metaphysics to add to Cudd's theory of oppression in order to eliminate her argument's circularity. In spite of challenges and criticisms that are brought against the capabilities approach formulated by Amartya Sen (1984) and Martha Nussbaum (2001), some of which I will discuss later in this chapter, I think the capabilities approach is a solid basis for the discussion and formulation of rights. Grounding the theory in this way not only responds to the circularity problem of Cudd's theory of oppression but also sheds light on the experiences of the Iranian American population and holds other merits that I will discuss shortly.

In my discussion, I suggest that we ground rights in capabilities instead of using other, more traditional methods of exploring this topic. People in general, and philosophers specifically, agree at least with the idea that some people have some rights. However, they disagree on what those rights actually are, where they come from, who has them, whether there are correlative duties, and whether rights are positive or negative (Gewirth 2001, 322). Whatever rights are, Rex Martin (2001, 26–27) argues, they are at least "fairly determinate things." This view of rights opposes Jack Donnelly's (1982, 42) view that rights are relative to a situation, such as whether a person deserves to have that right (for instance, does a convicted criminal have the right to remain free of prison?), or whether it is possible for the government to provide that right. I tend to agree with Martin that "rights are established ways of acting or being acted toward, or being treated."

The theories of rights are numerous and have been discussed extensively. I will discuss the three most prominent views on rights—rights as entitlements, rights as claims, and rights as wellbeing—and point out how the capabilities approach might answer some of the shortcomings and concerns stemming from each. Next, I will discuss the differing views on where rights come from (natural rights vs. civil rights). Last, I will show that the capabilities approach could answer many of the questions about rights raised here. If we ground rights in capabilities, we can know "what the motivating concerns [of rights] are and what the goal is" (Nussbaum 2001, 97). The objective is to raise everyone to the *threshold of functioning* with capabilities, rather than functioning, as our goal to allow for diversity in both planning one's life and conceptions of the good life (Sen 1992). This would give rights more force than mere rhetoric. For instance, if we claim that people have the right to food, but there is no feasible way for them to obtain food, the "right" is merely a hollow statement. In order to make this right a reality, we ought to facilitate "the 'four As': making healthy food *available*, delivering *assets* to obtain it, improving *abilities* to prepare it for consumption and creating *attitudes* that support its consumption" (Smith 2016, 179). Otherwise, it makes no sense to claim that a right to food exists. The U.S. Declaration of Independence declares the rights to "life, liberty, and the pursuit of happiness," but this promise is empty for some populations, including those who do not have access to proper nutrition.

Grounding Cudd's concept of harm in violations of capabilities, which are the basis for rights, provides a solid underpinning for what is wrong with injustice. It also recognizes oppression and suggests how to address it. The capabilities approach gives us guidelines for ensuring that citizens do, in fact, have rights and the means to actualize them. Capabilities answer the questions of what rights we have and what ought to be done about them; without this sort of grounding, rights remain ambiguous.

I will also analyze the Iranian American experience using the capabilities approach. There is little philosophical analysis on race that looks at the Iranian American population as a case study. The socio-economic status of Iranians in the United States, makes it difficult to understand this group as anything but privileged. Evaluating the situation of the Iranian American community via the capabilities approach will show how the harms caused by both microaggressions and cultural imperialism are substantial and have grave effects on the lives of those who experience them.

THE CAPABILITIES APPROACH

Capabilities are things that people are "actually able to do and to be" and must be preserved without damage, limited by the liberty principle (Nussbaum 2001, 5). This limitation to the capabilities is justified harm because "Not all actual human abilities exert a moral claim, only the ones that have been evaluated as valuable from an ethical viewpoint." Hence, Nussbaum claims that negative capabilities, such as the capability not to starve, should not be included in the list of capabilities that she proposes (Nussbaum, 2000a, 83). Nussbaum's list comprises capabilities that she believes will stand the best chance of universal consensus. I will start with a brief summary of her view and the justification for it before moving into the discussion of rights and capabilities.

The first three capabilities on the list are the most fundamental; without these three, others cannot be actualized. These are Life, Bodily Health, and Bodily Integrity. From these capabilities, we can derive the right to live a healthy, well-nourished life that does not end prematurely and that includes the right to reproductive health, freedom to move around free from physical and sexual violence, and freedom to enjoy sensual and sexual satisfaction (78). For instance, a person who is raped or forced into an arranged marriage has her capability of Bodily Integrity violated.

Next come Senses, Imagination and Thought, and Practical Reason. These capabilities allow individuals to become informed and provide the opportunity to develop their abilities to determine their comprehensive conception of the good and to plan their life, including education, religion, and artistic expressions (78–79). These include a person's ability to make critical decisions about their life. According to Nussbaum (2001), Practical Reason is one of the two most important capabilities because using it gives each person agency to make autonomous choices and determine their own path in life, instead of being herded as a "cog in a machine" (82). Governments that do not allow freedom of religion violate the capabilities of Thought and Practical Reason. Under such governments, we are deterred from developing our own conception of the good.

Capabilities that we use in the social aspects of life are Emotions, Affiliation, Other Species, Play, and Control over One's Political and Material Environment (Nussbaum 2001, 78–80). They include personal and social freedoms and opportunities as well as authority over one's life prospects. Freedom to develop friendships and other attachments, freedom to express emotions and joys, and freedom of political and economic associations and projects are part of this group. The capability of affiliation, alongside practical reason, is of special importance for Nussbaum. Like practical reason, the capability of affiliation holds special importance for Nussbaum because it underpins personal agency. At first glance, some of these capabilities listed might seem trivial or of less value than those mentioned earlier, but undermining them could be life-threatening. For example, under the government of the Islamic Republic of Iran or the Taliban, being joyful in public, smiling in government-issued photographs, or any display of play and happiness by teens and adults is stigmatized and often punished. This violates the capabilities of Play and Emotions. Youth suicide rates, alcoholism, and drug use in these societies are skyrocketing (See Hassanian-Moghaddam & Zamani 2017; Chegeni, et al. 2020; Hadid and Ghani 2019; Sadiqi 2018). Psychologists show that playing is essential to the mental and physical health of individuals, adults included (Brown, 2014). Being joyful and having the capability to play is crucial to a flourishing life. So, these capabilities are not trivial.

Nussbaum's list specifies many ways that people can potentially function to achieve a truly human life, but there might be relevant capabilities that Nussbaum does not name or that she is unaware of. I refer to those on her list as *capabilities* and those not on her list as *potential ways of functioning*. The distinction is merely between the capabilities Nussbaum identifies and others that might exist despite their absence from her list. These freedoms and opportunities must be constitutionally guaranteed for each individual person (rather than an aggregate of people). Nussbaum proposes these capabilities "as a foundation for basic political principles that should underwrite constitutional guarantees" (70–71).

The list of capabilities is merely a starting place for thinking about a theory of justice and drawing attention to what kind of rights are guaranteed. Sen does not provide a list of capabilities for our use; however, although he has not endorsed Nussbaum's list, he indeed refers to it. The list of capabilities, Nussbaum (2001, 71–72) argues, is intuitive in the sense that a thriving and flourishing life will include these capabilities and the opportunity for their development. She adds,

> The intuitive idea behind the approach is twofold: first, that certain functions are particularly central in human life, in the sense that their presence or absence is typically understood to be a mark of the presence or absence of human life; and second—this is what Marx found in Aristotle—that there is something that it is to do these functions in a truly human way, not merely an animal [non-human] way.

By *truly human,* Nussbaum refers to a life that is "*worthy* of a human being" (73). Nussbaum puts the individual in the center of her theory because her view of individuals is Kantian; each person is an end with the full value and dignity that each other person possesses. The acknowledgment of individuals' value and dignity has the potential to be life-changing for some people.

In a society in which human life is not always valued and some lives matter more, at least politically, the Kantian view of human value becomes a radical idea. The Trump administration's crackdown on illegal immigration, discouragement and imprisonment of asylum seekers, including forced (and long-lasting) separation of children from parents, makes one wonder how much dignity has been granted to the desperate people seeking refuge in the United States (Lanard 2019; Cheng 2018; Domonokse and Gonzales 2018). Although this is a bit of a digression, I want to point out that Kant died in 1804, yet preserving and observing human dignity is still a radical idea in 2020 in the United States. The capabilities approach puts individuals, not aggregates, in the center of evaluations of justice.

Nussbaum's list of capabilities is based on the likelihood that the capabilities would come out of an *overlapping consensus* among members of different cultures (Rawls 1993, 2000; Nussbaum 2001, 76). It would be hard to find a community that would not agree with the list provided by Nussbaum, regardless of their metaphysical view of the world. At the very least, Nussbaum's underlying assumption is that they wouldn't disagree (Nussbaum 74). To be sure, some cultures deny some of these capabilities to some of their populations; for instance, think about unequal pay, discrimination against differently abled bodies, the treatment of Native American populations in the United States, racism, and so on. Yet they would still agree that *people* are (or at least ought to be) better off having all of these capabilities, and that a life with these capabilities is better than one without them. Nussbaum captures these and many other liberties and freedoms with her list of capabilities and makes a strong case that the protection and promotion of capabilities should be a part of what justice requires.

What the Capabilities Approach is Not

The capabilities approach is not subjective welfarism. Both Nussbaum (2001) and Sen (1984) deny subjective welfarism, "the idea that each person's *perceived* wellbeing should be the basis for social choice" (Nussbaum 2001, 8; emphasis mine). An appeal to perceived wellbeing is not adequate, because our society, socioeconomic status, race, ability, and other characteristics shape our preferences, meaning that we might believe our needs are met when in reality they are not.

The capabilities approach does not use the utilitarian calculus in assessing the level of social justice in a society. We do not want to look at a sum, such as the gross national product (GNP) or an average per capita amount. "When we turn our attention from poverty to inequality [of capabilities], the multidimensionality of capability space has the potential to reveal important aspects of inequality that are missed by an exclusive focus on money metric" (Burchardt and Hick 2018, 44). Each individual's actual, not merely perceived, wellbeing ought to be considered. Individuals ought not to be considered as merely a contribution to the whole or as the very best judge of their own situation. Sen (2000, 59, 62) rules out the utilitarian approach as a way to access the level of justice and distribution of the goods in a society: "the utilitarian calculus tends to ignore inequalities in the distribution of happiness (only the sum total matters—no matter how unequally distributed)." Generally speaking, utilitarianism does not consider human rights, capabilities, or freedom and it does not yield any information on how *individuals* are doing.

The capabilities approach does not advocate for the equal treatment of each person, because people's needs differ in achieving the threshold of functioning. Under the capabilities approach, justice might require us to treat individuals unequally. Lorella Terzi (2005, 2007) gives a pertinent application of this theory to the case of children with physical and mental disabilities. She argues that differences in treatment are not only essential but also work within a theory of justice and equality.

Objections to the Capabilities Approach

Although this is not the place for a thorough discussion of the capabilities approach, a review of certain basic objections to this approach will clarify the approach and demonstrate its flexibility and resilience.

(1) The Capabilities and Wellbeing Objection

Nussbaum argues that all states ought to guarantee these capabilities in their laws. Some of the capabilities that she calls *basic capabilities* ought to come to the threshold of functioning—that is, there has to be a social minimum for everyone where everyone has the functioning level. Others are to be left at the threshold of functioning for people to decide which to develop—that is, some people might choose not to develop those capabilities but have the opportunity to do so if they so choose. Peter Vallentyne (2005) argues that the capabilities approach at best is nothing beyond wellbeing theory which evaluates justice based on the quality of life one lives. He adds that *all* capabilities ought to reach the level of functioning because if our goal is a good life for individuals, a life in which all of a person's capabilities are functioning is better than a life that merely has opportunities for functioning. We do not have a way to rate the value of the various capabilities, so it is "arbitrary to exclude some functioning that contributes to such value [be it good life or other things]" (362–363). There are two points to be made here. First, Vallentyne misses the notion of autonomy. My life is improved by the capability to learn how to sing well. Even if I do not choose to pursue the development of that attribute, I still like having it as an option in the future. However, I do not want to be forced to bring that capability to functioning. That would be a violation of my autonomy and would not lead to a good life. So, to say that we ought to be concerned with the level of functioning for all capabilities, as Vallentyne does, would be to say that people ought to be forced to develop capabilities to the level of functioning even when they do not want to do so. Second, we are not *arbitrarily* picking from the capabilities to get them to functioning level. Rather, the basic capabilities are necessary for the development of the others. Therefore, Vallentyne's argument that the capabilities approach and the wellbeing approach are equivalent does not hold. Consider his argument (368), presented below with my responses.

P1. Capabilities are opportunities to function.

My response: Capabilities are not "opportunities," but rather ways that we can be. I might have the capability of being politically active and create affiliations but not the opportunity to get it to the functioning level. For instance, I might have the capability of running for the elected office of Oklahoma governor, but not the opportunity to get this capability to the level of functioning. So, it is false to say that capabilities are "opportunities to function." Instead, they are ways of being that we should have the opportunity to bring to the functioning level.

P2. No functionings are irrelevant to justice (justice is not concerned solely with basic capabilities).

My response: This premise is false. Justice is certainly concerned with all capabilities, but not necessarily with their functioning, because not everyone desires to fulfill all their capabilities. To force people to do so would be a violation of their autonomy and grounds for questioning.

P3. Opportunities are to be understood as effective freedoms and not merely as control freedom. Note: "Effective freedom to function includes all possible functioning independently of whether one's will plays any role in bringing them about. . . . Control freedom to function is based on those possible functionings that one can bring about, or at least sufficiently influence the probability of coming about, through the appropriate exercise of one's will" (Vallentyne 2005, 363). That is, having effective freedom means that regardless of what I desire, those freedoms will exist. However, control freedom refers to freedoms that I can bring about because I will or desire them and work towards achieving them. Under effective freedom, Vallentyne gives us the example of a person who is in a coma. Although she might have the will to eat, she lacks the control to feed herself. If others feed her, she has effective freedom.

My response: First, I do not believe that the coma example is very clear because the person's will is unknown. However, suppose she had in the past mentioned that she did not wish to be fed if she were ever in a coma. So, she has both control and effective freedom. However, if she indeed desires to be fed, she has both freedoms. Further, if we force someone to do things that they do not want, we are infringing on their autonomy and ways of life. Suppose I do not want to own home furniture. I find furniture arrogant, useless, and classist. I would find it intrusive if someone appeared at my house with a truck full of furniture as a gift for me. So long as I am not violating the liberty principle, and owning furniture is something I am able to do but choose not to, I ought not be forced to do so. This is a crucial point that Vallentyne seems to overlook.

P4. The opportunity for the wellbeing approach is committed to evaluating opportunities on the basis of their contribution to *wellbeing* (quality of life . . .). As does capabilities approach p1–p3.

My response: The capabilities and wellbeing approaches are equivalent.

Vallentyne does not fully do justice to the nuances of the capabilities approach and merely reduces it to the wellbeing approach. For the reasons given in my responses to the premises, I think that his argument fails.

It is interesting to note that Vallentyne criticizes the capabilities approach for not promoting functioning for all capabilities, but others criticize Nussbaum for demanding that all governments, even non-liberal ones, bring everyone above the level of functioning.

(2) The Universalism Objection

Nussbaum's capabilities approach has been criticized for being universalist. The critics argue that expecting non-liberal governments to guarantee her list of capabilities in their constitution is nothing but imperialism and arrogant intrusion on their freedom. Hilary Charlesworth (2000) argues that "The development of international law relied on European ideals as universals and these standards were imposed by colonialism and conquest" (74). In many cases, such imposition has harmed the colonized people. Examples of such cases are practically endless, but the one that hits closest to home is the colonization of Africa and North America. Charlesworth's concern merits consideration. She is right to be concerned about imposing Western values on those who disagree with us. However, she ignores some ethically relevant distinctions. Not every universal value (or its imposition) is a violation of one's cultural autonomy or a nation's sovereignty. People's demand for equal rights in non-western societies has often been criticized as being "western."

Some societies consider educating girls and women to be wrong, believing that a woman's job, her proper destiny and fulfillment, is to be a wife and mother. But, clearly, a society that enforces this vision puts women in a disadvantaged position in relation to men and limits their choices immensely. It is not imperialistic to apply universal values to issues regarding discrimination based on sex and gender within family life. It is a moral demand to allow all people to live full human lives and have the opportunity to make authentic (and informed) choices. This is different from colonialism, in which people are forced to serve a colonial power.

In her paper "Missionary Positions," Ann Cudd (2005, 166) gives us two responses to this kind of charge. First, she argues that we must make distinctions between imperialism, "missionism," Eurocentrism, and humanism.

> (1) imperialism, which seeks to impose a universal standard that merely serves the interests of the imperial power; (2) "missionism," which attempts to change the deepest spiritual commitments of the subjects of the work; (3) Eurocentrism (Americentrism?), which imposes its aesthetic and cultural norms on others; and (4) humanism, which tries to help the oppressed find a path out of their oppression.

Of the four, humanism is the only justified method of intervening into another's culture. In the other three situations, the intervening nation, which Cudd calls "invaders," do not have the right intentions. For a group to justly intervene in another group's way of living, they must have the right intentions, their strategy ought to be effective, and the outcome ought to be considered (167–168). Imperialists, missionaries, Eurocentrics, and humanists might all have the same goal in mind, but their intentions differ, and that makes a moral difference. The intentions behind humanism make it distinct from, and superior to, imperialism. Imperialists invade with their own benefits in mind, using physical and material force. Humanists cannot be equated with imperialists because imperialism "is not simply an attitude, but involves real, material injury from which psychological injuries may well follow" (Cudd 2005, 169). The accusations against Nussbaum's capabilities approach are therefore not founded, because she does not have imperialist intentions or methods. Nussbaum does not believe that we ought to force people to develop each of their capabilities; rather, she believes that the opportunity for their development ought to be guaranteed by every constitution.

Second, Cudd rightly argues that "the postcolonial theorists assume a mistaken essentialist notion of culture" (166). But cultures are fluid and ever-changing. Iranian culture is different in the United States from in Iran. It is also different in Iran now from when I left in 1988. Fights for women's rights, children's rights, and other social and political rights are ongoing works of (internal) activists. Changing certain aspects of culture to bring about equality does not imply that all parts of the culture are wrong and should be changed.

Traditional cultures seem to be most concerned about the status of women in their society and how the West affects their choices and ways of life. Pointing out to women that they live oppressed lives as virtual slaves to their families could certainly cause chaos, confusion, and even inspire popular feminist insurrection in the hope of breaking through the systematic forces that keep them caged. Yet although the dissemination of universalist values is destabilizing, as it has been even in the West, it generally has positive effects in the end. This is not a violation of cultural autonomy but a prerequisite for it. Cultures are the activities of people. To be autonomous is to make choices that are not made under duress. People are not able to make autonomous choices if they are not given a choice, or if one that is given to them is not one even worth considering.

Nussbaum's view is not one that condemns traditional roles, be they in western or nonwestern societies. However, she argues that "if women fully in possession of the capabilities on the list want to choose a traditional gender-divided mode of life . . . any good political liberalism should create spaces for them to do so" (2000a, 123). One might argue that the women in the western liberal world are also faced with many obstacles and that the choices they make do not always lead to flourishing. This is true. However, we have a great many choices regarding career, mate, education, and reproduction. Having options might cause confusion and anxiety, but anxiety about making the right decision for ourselves is certainly far superior than the anxiety, even despair, of having no choice in our lives. Nussbaum (2001, 42) writes:

> We should say, first, that if divorce and career difficulties are painful, as they surely are, they are a lot less painful than being unable to work when one is starving because one will be beaten if one goes outdoors, or being unable to leave an abusive marriage because of illiteracy and lack of employment skills.

Here, Nussbaum is referring to women in India, where a woman who loses her husband often suffers malnutrition, starvation, injury, or even death. In some villages, the husband's family might cause her physical harm if she tries to find work to survive (Nussbaum 15–24). For many people, divorce is one of the most difficult experiences of their lives, but even worse is having one's life or health endangered by living in a physically (or emotionally) abusive marriage.

Below is a list of Nussbaum's responses to objections of cultural imperialism or charges of insensitivity to others' legitimate claims to self-determination.

1. We specify the list at a rather high level of generality, leaving a lot of room for nations to specify the items in accordance with their history and their current problems.
2. We make capabilities and not functioning the appropriate political goal.
3. We put the various liberties, and choice itself, in a place of prominence on the list.
4. We interpret the whole list as a list of capabilities to be promoted for political purposes, a core that can be the object of an overlapping consensus of many distinct conceptions, not as a fully comprehensive conception of the good.
5. On the whole, we leave implementation to the internal political processes of each republican state. Thus, we are advising and not requiring. (Nussbaum 2001, 105).

Additionally, Charlesworth warns that we should be hesitant to talk about universal civil and political rights to women in developing countries because their economic plight is a more pressing concern. The worries we have in a liberal democratic society are very different. She puts it this way:

> The search for universal women's predicaments can obscure differences among women and homogenize women's experiences. Feminists from the developing world often charge Western feminists with being overly concerned with the acquisition of civil and political rights while ignoring the significance of economic and social rights, such as the right to food and to housing, or collective rights such as the right to self-determination and development. (Charlesworth 2000, 73)

Charlesworth seems to assume that when we talk about women's rights in a universal context, we are ignoring their basic needs for food, housing, or collective rights. Nussbaum repudiates this. The rights that Charlesworth has mentioned here will not be actualized unless women gain the opportunity to develop the capabilities necessary to ensure these rights.

Some governments cannot ensure that everyone has access to food in all situations, but they can create and maintain policies, institutions, and programs that ensure people's development of the capabilities required to access what John Rawls refers to as primary goods. Primary goods are "various social conditions and all-purpose means that are generally necessary to enable citizens adequately to develop and fully exercise their moral powers, and to pursue their determinate conceptions of the good" (Rawls 2003, 57). These goods help people become morally equal members of society with full capability to cooperate in social and political life.

Both Sen and Nussbaum agree that there is a very tight correlation between primary goods and capabilities. According to Nussbaum (2000a), the list of primary goods includes both "thing-like terms and capability-like terms," but she uses them in terms of capabilities (126). Sen asserts that Rawls's theory seeks the capabilities, even though Rawls might have intended otherwise. "[Rawls] motivates the focus on primary goods by discussing what the primary goods enable people to do. It is only because of his assumption—often implicit—that the same mapping of primary goods to capabilities holds for all, that he can sensibly concentrate on primary goods rather than on corresponding capabilities" (Sen 1984, 320). In other words, Rawls's "primary goods" are really just another way of describing capabilities. The list of primary goods is a list of what people need to get to the basic level of functioning. Without these things, we would not have much opportunity to develop our own comprehensive conception of the good. Thus, the capabilities approach does not ignore the basic needs of people in the developing countries. The basic capabilities are primary and essential for the development of others.

(3) The Liberal Philosophy and Choice Objection

Anne Phillips (2001) argues that Nussbaum's version of feminist internationalism is built on the significance of choice in liberal philosophy but implies that the choice of inequality would be somehow irrational. She adds that Nussbaum condemns decisions that leave us in unequal positions. Admittedly, I agree that choices of inequality are not ideal, but they are often the products of autonomous choices; hence, my view on voluntary oppression. However, in my view, inequality can be chosen, but an acceptable inequality should be the result of informed, educated, uncoerced choice. It is possible that informed, educated, and free people will choose to live as unpaid homemakers —consider cases of Iranian American immigrant women who choose the safety of their home over the unknown world of employment in a new country. Nussbaum's approach leaves open this course of action. However, when a woman is content with having no formal education, no legal right to divorce, and no social right to work, and knows that she will face beatings and even starvation if she rejects the inferior status and condition imposed on her society, we have legitimate grounds to doubt that her acquiescence is a free choice (Nussbaum 2001, 77). Does she have a free or autonomous choice? Would she have chosen another sort of life if these extreme conditions did not exist? It is possible, perhaps even probable. Choices made under such harsh conditions and perilous alternatives are suspicious. Iranian Americans thrive in the United States. We have access to education, legal rights, freedom of movement, and (depending on our immigration status) many other freedoms that most other Americans enjoy. We are grateful for the opportunities and tend to minimize discriminatory experiences. Yet we typically remain politically unengaged—even refraining from affiliating with a political party—to avoid perpetuating negative stereotypes against us, because becoming politically engaged presents significantly worse consequences.

Under the capabilities approach, the government should not set unjustified limitations on our ability to develop our lives and our capabilities. Of course, we might decide to limit our own capabilities or choose not to develop some of them, but that ought to be an informed choice. Nussbaum is not necessarily concerned with lack of choice but rather lack of free choice. Some free choices are due to internalized expectations of inferiority. If we are convinced that we are somehow inferior to others, we could be oppressed even though our choices are free. So, if one makes choices based on false consciousness, one is making a free choice based on adaptive preferences.

(4) The Threshold Objection

Richard Arneson (2000, 56) raises the next objection. He argues that the idea of "threshold" is arbitrary and cannot be justifiably instituted. He lays out one form of the problem this way:

> One difficulty is how one nonarbitrarily sets the threshold level. Why here and not higher or lower? What we have is a smooth continuum of possible levels of overall capability for flourishing. Higher capability is always better than lower capability. But I do not see how much any unique level (not even a broad thick line) can be picked out such that if a person has that level, she has "enough."

There are three concerns we face with setting thresholds: first, on the individual level, Arneson is concerned that we must draw the threshold level arbitrarily because each individual's level is different. But this is really an empirical issue, to be determined for each individual, in the context of our resources; it is not a theoretical problem. Second is the problem of determining what is sufficient generally, because a better capability for flourishing is always preferable. This, again, stems from a misunderstanding of the empirical element. If each individual is able to make autonomous choices as effectively as resources allow, we have succeeded in securing their basic capabilities. Third, some capabilities are basic, and others are not. Why should our constitutional guarantees include the basic level of the capabilities spectrum and exclude the non-basic capabilities? The answer is that what Arneson terms the "lower" capabilities are necessary for developing the "higher" ones. Each person will have the opportunity to develop their own talents, capabilities, and conception of the good. Once their capabilities exceed the threshold, there is no limit to their development.

Moreover, Arneson is concerned that Nussbaum does not give us clear guidelines on what is required to get people to the desired level. Nussbaum responds that "this [setting a threshold] is best done by internal processes of each liberal democracy, as it interprets its own constitution. History shows that this is not only possible but is also quite a reasonable way to balance concerns for history and culture against the demands of a universal norm" (Nussbaum 2000a, 126). So, each government decides how much it is able to do (economically and culturally) to achieve the fullest opportunities for capability development. The historical and cultural aspects of each society must also be considered. Consequently, for a pre-democratic culture that does not yet highly value the capability of political affiliation, the threshold would be set below that of a culture that openly encourages its citizens to participate in politics. However, Nussbaum (127) adds that "Levels should be set high enough to goad people to take intelligent action, but they should not be set so high as to bring the whole document into discredit." No basic human functioning capability should be destroyed or undermined unless a government is utterly incapable of makings those guarantees.

(5) The Group Membership Objection

The last concern one might have addresses the capabilities approach in relation to our criteria of oppression set in chapter 3. The worry is that a theory of oppression based on the capabilities approach requires us to forgo the criteria of group membership. But this objection does not apply to my theory because, although it is individual-based (each person must have the constitutional guarantees based on the capabilities), it does not contradict our group membership criterion. We can recognize the oppression of a group if an individual's capabilities are thwarted due to the fact that they belong to a particular group.

In responding to the objections, I have used the capabilities approach to shed light on the nature of oppression. The capabilities approach is well-suited to this; it focuses on the site of oppression, the individual, and reveals a vast range of morally important characteristics of the individual, all of which play powerful roles in allowing us to describe exactly how oppression occurs and what its remedies might be. As long as governments guarantee the development of these capabilities to the threshold of functioning, we can get closer to a society that is just and beneficial to its members. The capabilities approach shifts the focus away from society as a whole and toward the individual, where it belongs. A country might have a high GNP but also be plagued by poverty due to government corruption or lack of concern for its citizens' living standards. The capabilities approach looks at individuals' lives to determine if the society is just.

Once a government guarantees these capabilities, we ought to be free to choose to develop any of our capabilities and other ways of functioning. If a person violates the development of another individual's capabilities, they have violated the liberty principle, so the society [or the government] is justified in curtailing that person's development of capabilities. As Nussbaum points out, not all capabilities ought to be guaranteed by the constitution. For instance, the capability to commit atrocities is not protected. However, we are able to express freedom of speech although it might be offensive to some groups. So, to harm is to violate the capabilities that one is entitled to develop (which, as mentioned, are those that do not violate the liberty principle).

The capabilities approach is a good basis for the discussion of rights. In the next section, I will argue that capabilities generate rights. The capabilities approach best answers many of the questions we might have about what rights are, who has them, and so forth. So, in essence, harm is violation of one's rights, which are generated by capabilities.

CAPABILITIES AS RIGHTS-GENERATING

I want to erect a bridge between rights and capabilities. I will argue that capabilities generate rights. For example, if I have the capability to be involved in politics, I ought to have the right to do so (as far as it does not violate others' rights). We must work on understanding the connection (or relationship) between rights and capabilities, but capabilities are a better way to talk about human situations than are rights (Williams 1987). In addition, discussions of capabilities are typically more concrete than discussions of rights. The capabilities approach to rights starts with what we can do and be as humans and what leads to flourishing human lives, and ends with what rights we ought to have. I want to draw rights from capabilities, whereas Nussbaum wants to keep rights and capabilities as separate dialogues. However, she is correct to point out that "thinking in terms of capabilities gives us a benchmark as we think about what it is to secure a right to someone" (2001, 98). We start with capabilities that people have the opportunity to develop and see what that means for them and how they put those capabilities to work. We can then see what the government ought to aim for regarding citizens' flourishing while they decide what rights they should grant. Other scholars have either argued for grounding rights in the capabilities approach or have used the capabilities approach to inform an analysis that yields a moral grounding for rights (Venkatapuram, 2014; Smith 2016; Loots and Walker 2016; Nelson 2004; Ibrahim and Tiwari 2014).

Although Nussbaum, as noted above, argues that capabilities should be the basis on which a society is judged, she does not want to eliminate rights talk altogether for the following four reasons. (1) Because we are familiar with rights talk, it helps place our attention on people's claims to just treatment by their government and (2) to just claims to certain things (freedoms, liberties, prerogatives, privileges, etc.) by virtue of being human. She asserts that the talk of rights gets more attention than the talk of capabilities. Further, (3) when we talk of rights, it often entails the importance of choice and autonomy, concepts that capabilities talk does not immediately bring to mind. Last (4), although people disagree about the *status* of rights, there seem to be agreements about *having* rights (Nussbaum 2001, 100–101). In short, Nussbaum persists with rights language because it is familiar, whereas the details of the capabilities approach are still being worked out.

Sen, too, continues with the concept of rights, but he looks at them from a different angle. He believes that "[p]olitical rights are important not only for the fulfillment of needs, they are crucial also for the formulation of needs" (38). In other words, for Sen, political rights help people identify and express their needs. But I disagree with this. In my view, people identify and express their needs not according to the rights that they have (or believe they have), but according to their need to develop a flourishing life with full dignity and human value, which includes being able to decide and live by one's own comprehensive conception of the good. Therefore, Sen's dichotomy of rights and capabilities is unnecessary, because capabilities are the building blocks of rights.

RIGHTS: ENTITLEMENTS, CLAIMS, OR WELLBEING

Next, I will briefly describe the conceptions of rights as entitlements, rights as claims, and rights as wellbeing, pointing out deficiencies in each view and situating my own view among the three.

Rights as Entitlements

Robert Nozick (1974, 92) defined rights as "permissions to do something and correlative obligations of others not to interfere," which only gives us the obligation not to interfere. In other words, "rights are entitlements, expressing certain ways that people may *not* treat one another" (Smith 1992, 220). Libertarians generally assert that the only time that we have legitimate ground for coercion is to prevent our own freedom from being violated. So, for instance, if I am entitled to free speech, it does not follow that people ought to provide me with a "soapbox," but rather that they must not stop me from climbing onto *my* soapbox (Peffer 1978, 66, 68). This view entitles me to negative rights only, whereas the capabilities approach gives us access to both positive and negative rights.

Tara Smith (1992) raises several objections to positive rights. First, she argues that rights are not to be looked at as providing a complete moral (social justice) theory but merely "one component of a complete moral theory" (222). Having the right to do x, doesn't mean that a person ought to do x, or it is a morally appropriate behavior. Those are separate questions. Second, Smith argues that having welfare rights would "handcuff people to one another's desires" in order to make sure that people are able to exercise their rights (Smith, 225). This is an unfair burden for Smith because it will limit people to what other people might need/want because we ought to constantly consider others as we choose our actions. These objections will be pertinent to my discussion of rights as entitlement.

The capabilities approach protects people from "potential intrusion," among other things. It also accounts for differences in circumstances, biology, and luck because, due to these and other factors, some people need more resources than others to get to the functioning level. If justice requires that everyone have the same opportunities, then we ought to level the playing field by accounting for inequalities that hinder a person's development of capabilities. Rights without positive obligations on others to protect them are meaningless. Providing only negative rights to a starving child or an elderly person who is unable to get the medication that he or she needs could leave them dead (Shue 1980). They ought to have a positive right to food and medicine, and for this right to make a difference in their life, some other person or government entity must take action. Libertarians disagree with positive rights—having a right does not mean that one can exercise that right. In the United States, at present, having a right does not always come with a guarantee that one can exercise that right. Under the capabilities approach, when we have a right, we ought also to have the preconditions necessary to exercise it.

Tara Smith (1992, 225) argues that "a right to freedom does not promise unlimited abilities to use one's freedom to satisfy all of one's desires." But no one is making such a claim. For many reasons, we all agree that neither individuals nor governments ought to be tied to people's desires. First, some desires might be violent and may violate others' rights. Second, the welfarists do not claim that *all* of our desires ought to be satisfied; rather, they aim to fulfill basic needs (such as food and water) so we can exercise other rights. For example, consider the right to receive K-12 education. According to the entitlement theory of rights, no one is responsible to provide people with the means to exercise the right to education, which means that children who do not have access to school materials or transportation are unable to exercise their right to receive K-12 education. Social justice requires that we have the ability to exercise our rights in general. If rights are merely words on a document, and they do not actually change lives and improve people's opportunities, they do not benefit anyone. However, the capabilities approach does not imply that one has the right to have every desire fulfilled. On the contrary, the government's job ought to be to situate people so they will not have to be dependent on one another so they can make free, autonomous choices and not be enslaved by their needs. People cannot live free lives if their most basic needs are not met, but Smith does not believe that we should be concerned about this.

Perhaps the most outrageous defense of libertarian theories of rights is Smith's (1992, 233) claim that "it is undeniable that some people's freedom 'buys them less stuff'." In other words, a negative rights theory is "harmful" only insofar as it creates disparities in how much "stuff" people own. This appears outrageous (as it should) to those who care about justice. Furthermore, for Smith, claiming that a poor person does not have the right to medicine if he cannot exercise it is the same as saying "that a poor person is unfree because she is not allowed to steal" (232). But these claims are clearly different. Stealing is the act of taking someone's property without their consent. Under no view of rights, including the capabilities approach, does anyone have the right to steal from or harm another person if it is not in the case of self-defense or defense of another—unless Smith considers taxation as stealing from the citizens, which is a discussion that goes beyond the scope of. In some circumstances, the right to medicine is essential to exercise one's right to life. The government's job is, at the very least, to protect its citizens' lives. Providing medicine to a poor person who is unable to do so himself counts as protection of life. This obligates the government to provide medicine (a positive right) and not merely allow people to acquire it (a negative right).

Rights ought not to be only for the middle class, upper class, or social elite. Demanding that the government provide basic health care, education, and adequate protection of citizens is not an argument for communism. We do not have to have a communist society in order to ensure equal basic needs for everyone and to make sure everyone starts from a level playing field. It is worth pointing out that communist nations have been unable to achieve what I am arguing for here. Cudd (2006, 122–125) points out that, in a capitalist society such as ours, we have more resources to bring people to a better state of existence.

Finally, according to Ronald Dworkin, the entitlement view of rights "uses rather than explains the concept of a right" (1978, 80). It does not really tell us what rights are; rather, the theory merely tells us what it would be like to practice our rights. I think Dworkin is onto something. If we take capabilities as the basis of rights, we can use entitlement theory as actually having a concept of rights and, in addition, entitling people to positive as well as negative rights. That is not what Nozick and Smith had in mind, but their entitlement theory can also be extended to entitle us to positive rights and the freedom to exercise them. We could have a hybrid of positive rights and entitlements that *stems from* the capabilities approach, but that is not the traditional understanding of entitlement theory. Left-wing entitlement theories can be articulated in conjunction with the capabilities approach to entitle us to positive rights. By "left-wing entitlement theory" I mean a theory of distributive justice that gives rights to x for the person who has the capability to do x.

Rights as Claims

Rights as claims entails that "[l]egal claim-rights are necessarily the grounds of other people's duties toward the right-holder ... [and] rights are necessarily linked with the duties of other people" (Feinberg 1973, 58, 62). This is closer to the capabilities view than the entitlement theory of rights. The issues surrounding the claims theory of rights include (1) what it means to have a claim, (2) what duty correlates with it, and (3) who has this obligation and to what extent it reaches. I will try to explore some of these problems here. I will start with Rex Martin's concern about the vagueness of the notion of a claim.

Martin (1993, 55) asks if having a claim to something is merely having one's concerns heard. Having one's concerns heard is the beginning of having a claim, which leads to an investigation about whether the claim is valid. When "a threshold of satisfaction [of a valid claim] has actually been achieved, the claim becomes a valid *claim-to*. It has then become the ground of other people's duties." The claim-to is a necessary condition for claim-against, which gives other people duties and obligations. That is, if one person has a right, then someone else has a duty towards the right holder based on this right.

Let's consider the case of someone having the right not to be lied to (Montague 1980). According to Phillip Montague, if we have an obligation not to lie to someone, then that person has the right not to be lied to. Montague finds this unacceptable and unfounded.

> For even if, say, the obligation not to lie to others implies that others have a right not to be lied to, the right not to be lied to is not the *ground* of the obligations not to lie. One cannot *justify* the judgment that A is obligated not to lie to B by stating that B has a right not to be lied to, because the two statements are logically equivalent [equivalency dilemma]. Thus, even if a statement concerning one individual's obligation to another implies a statement about the second in-

dividual's right against the first, it does not follow that the rights-statement can serve as either a justification or explanation of the obligation-statement. (375)

Hence, we need another basis to justify obligations that we have based on these rights, because the rights and the obligations say the same thing. If we say that what justifies the obligation is the right that it correlates to, we are begging the question. The capabilities approach addresses this concern. It looks at people's capabilities (which are the basis of rights) and decides others' obligation. Under the capabilities approach, we have the capability of being reasonable and making rational decisions for ourselves. If we are lied to, then we cannot make the decisions we would have made for ourselves if we were told the truth. So, being lied to would violate one's capability to make rational decisions based on the facts of the matter. Our capabilities are justified by the fact that they lead to flourishing human lives. (I will say more on this later in the chapter.)

Martin (1993, 78) argues against having a duty if one is not, and cannot be, aware of one's duties. He states: "if one cannot even be aware of a particular reason for doing one's duty, or cannot credit it as a good reason, then one cannot be said to have a duty to act for that reason. That particular reason can make no claim on that person's duty." Here, I think Martin is mistaking the epistemic question "can I know all of my duties?" with the question "what duties do I have?" He is right in asserting that we might not know all of our duties and obligations. But knowing my duties is different from simply having those duties. Additionally, he conflates the epistemic question with the culpability question. If I do not know what duties I have, I cannot be responsible (or morally culpable) for not performing them. However, it does not follow that I do not have that duty. Martin attempts to respond to concerns such as these, but I do not believe that he adequately deals with the issue. He clarifies that,

> I am not arguing here that people have only the duties they believe themselves to have. . . . [T]hey can properly be held to be under a *moral* duty which they do not now believe themselves to be under if the argument for that duty can be constructed from the overall social set of moral beliefs they do have (subject, of course, to the constraint that this particular construction is not blocked by *other* important beliefs they have, for example, by their scientific or religious beliefs.) My point, then is that people can have only the duties that they are reflectively able to have. (79)

He raises a legitimate concern. Suppose that under no amount of reflection can I see that it is my duty to provide adequate food and shelter for my child, despite having the means available to me. Perhaps I have little gift for intellectual analysis. It does not follow that I do not have the duties that I cannot know I have towards my child. At best, it means that I am not culpable if I do not provide these necessities for my child. I think we are left with the question of whether acting on ignorance makes us morally culpable. Martin's view is that if there are no circumstances in which I can know my duty, then I do not have one. My view is that I do, but I am not culpable if I do not fulfill my duties. My ignorance might not make me culpable, but it does not make me dutiful either. So, to have a duty and to know that you have certain duties are two different matters to be dealt with separately.

Rights as *valid claims-to and -against* is closer to the capabilities approach than is the traditional understanding of rights as entitlements. With the list of capabilities that Nussbaum gives us, we are situated to see what people are capable of doing and help them get to the level at which they can use their capabilities to pursue the lives they desire. If a person has a claim-to and a claim-against something, such as decision-making jurisdiction over her reproductive health, the government has a duty to assure that she has the means to achieve that right. In this case, that refers to the right to decide regarding her own reproductive health. That might mean freely accessible information about birth control, available and affordable birth control for those who cannot afford it, sex education classes in schools, an absence of forced sterilization and forced pregnancies, and so forth. The capabilities approach can account for the claims view by clarifying people's rights and duties.

Rights as Wellbeing

Rights to wellbeing stem "directly from the concept of human worth and involve the guaranteed satisfaction of basic human needs" (Peffer 1978, 79). At the basis of rights as wellbeing is the idea of human dignity and worth. Joel Feinberg (1970, 252) agrees that human dignity sets people as "potential maker[s] of claims." The wellbeing view of rights obligates us to provide social goods in order to recognize human dignity and value. This is a consequentialist understanding of rights, and its goal is to make people's lives better, but the wellbeing theory of rights alone is not adequate for a full list of rights. "'[R]ights to well-being' is not an all-inclusive category for any right to any benefit we may have (many of these will be social and economic rights which are social contract rights but not rights to well-being . . .)" (Peffer 1970, 79). He adds that we need both the social contract and wellbeing theories of rights to account for the satisfaction of non-basic rights, such as the right to free speech. He categorizes some rights as rights to personal wellbeing (such as the right to health care) and others as political rights (such as the right to free speech).

My view of rights is based not on the social contract, but rather on what makes a flourishing human life grounded on the development of one's human capabilities. The social contract is not the justification for political rights, because those rights are only those that we have agreed to and not necessarily what people need in order to live flourishing lives. These agreements can be subjective. Further, not everyone is present when agreements are made. The interest and needs of the disenfranchised might be left out of the discussion. Lawmakers instead should use capabilities to guide political rights, because this approach aims at flourishing human lives. Social contract theory, on the other hand, assumes merely that we agree to certain rights that everyone wishes to have. The capabilities approach is more specific; it provides a list that Nussbaum claims everyone would agree on.

Rights as wellbeing aims to actually improve people's lives. That is, this view presupposes that people should be guaranteed a certain level of flourishing. In other words, rights are important not merely because people have them, but because they actually do the work of improving people's lives. The intention behind the rights-as-wellbeing view is benevolent. However, sometimes it is not possible to know what is in a person's best interests or what serves their welfare best, and sometimes people have "objectives other than personal wellbeing. If, for example, a person fights successfully for a cause, making great personal sacrifice (even perhaps giving his or her life for it), then this may be a big agency [personal] achievement without being a corresponding achievement of personal wellbeing" (Sen 1987, 28). Further, "sources other than the nature of one's life" can affect one's wellbeing (27). For instance, one might be ill or lose a loved one. Although illness and grief decrease wellbeing and have severe negative effects on our personal lives, these adverse circumstances are of a different nature from the absence of social and political rights. No bill of rights can eliminate illness and grief from human lives. So the realm of human flourishing addressed by rights is clearly not coextensive with the entire range of human wellbeing. In other words, much of what is required for wellbeing falls outside the realm of rights that governments can guarantee.

The capabilities approach uses people's wellbeing as one guiding factor but not as the highest priority, because personal factors in wellbeing (such as illness and grief) are often beyond the control of governments. Some people might be unable to achieve wellbeing even if all of their capabilities are met and developed to the functioning level. Under the capabilities approach, we are concerned with establishing constitutional grounds that enable people to develop and use their capabilities. This is likely to increase individuals' wellbeing, but does not guarantee it, nor does it claim to do so. Some elements of wellbeing are simply beyond anyone's control. The best we can do is level the field to give individuals access to the same opportunities and privileges.

In summary, I have discussed three theories of rights: rights as entitlements, rights as claims, and rights as wellbeing. These cover three questions. (1) What does it mean to say "I have a right to x"? (2) What justifies my claim to a right to x? (3) What rights do I have (and particularly, do I have positive rights)? Smith (1992) and Feinberg (1970) address question (1), and Nussbaum (2001) addresses (2) and (3), but I aim to show that the capabilities view can address all three. I also believe that the capabilities approach can avoid the shortcomings of each view, as I have discussed throughout, so it would be best to reject each of these views and start with the capabilities approach. Capabilities give us what we need if we are committed to justice and equality: a guaranteed equal opportunity for a flourishing life.

In the next section, I will discuss the two kinds of human rights and address the question of by what virtue we have the rights that we have.

JUSTIFYING RIGHTS

There are, generally speaking, two kinds of human rights: natural rights and civil rights. Natural rights are those that people have by virtue of being human. So, we all have them. This idea comes from the notion that humans are more or less equal. Civil rights, on the other hand, are legitimate claims by citizens of a state against a legitimate government as well as against other citizens. Civil rights discussions raise the question of what makes a government legitimate. If a government meets our legitimacy criteria, then the rights it gives are the ones that we are entitled to. Although people in general seem to be committed to this notion, it has several problems (Hobbes 1985; Rousseau 1987; Locke 1980). First, people disagree about what makes a government legitimate. Second, even if we agree on this, we may question why we are granted certain rights and not others. Imagine a democratically elected government that does not recognize its citizens' right to freedom of religion. Although the government is legitimate, it is not infallible; no government is. Governments make mistakes and sometimes do not grant rights that we should have based on our human value. The U.S. Constitution is an agreement between the government and the citizens. As long as the constitution requires that the government be democratically elected, and as long as the government respects and upholds the constitution, the government is legitimate. We are to agree then, that if the government meets these two criteria, then it is legitimate. However, even when a group of people are democratically elected and meet all the legitimacy criteria, they might still be oppressive and fail to grant the most basic human rights. Under the capabilities approach, the constitution should guarantee a list of capabilities that, at a minimum, include those given by Nussbaum. I should note that if the government does not have the means to guarantee a right (such as education for all, or clean water) for anyone, that government is not necessarily oppressive, although they might be poor or lack other resources and means to provide that right. This would answer the question of what rights we have and which the government should grant us. This rights-based capabilities approach is a version of natural rights theory.

As mentioned earlier, natural rights are those that we have by virtue of our humanity. Theist supporters of natural rights theory typically argue that our rights are God-given, as does the preamble to the U.S. Constitution. This view of natural rights stems from Locke, who believed that we have some rights beyond the right to self-preservation, not because of a government or a civil society, but by virtue of being human and being creations of God. Locke (1980, 66) claims that all people have a right to "life, liberty, and property." Further, Locke argued that in addition to the right to life, we have the right to our property and to punish those who break the law. According to Locke, although there is justice, morality, and the right to punishment in the state of nature, because the nature of punishment is unclear people agree to a government to set judges, laws, and enforcers. So, Locke believes that we have rights in the state of nature, but we should have a government to codify and uphold them. Like Hobbes, Locke is a contractarian, but his view of rights is based on natural rights rather than civil rights because, in his view, we have many rights in the state of nature.

Natural rights theory poses some epistemic questions. If our rights are God-given, we might ask what rights God gave us. If, on the other hand, we have rights by virtue of being human, then we must wonder which ones they are. Whichever way we define the origin of natural rights, we are left with the epistemic question of what rights are. The capabilities approach resembles natural rights theory but gets around the epistemic concerns.

In my view, the rights we have are those that we possess the capability to actualize. Although we have the capability to destroy, harm, or commit acts of atrocities, we do not have the right to do these things because they violate others' development of their capabilities. So, rights come from certain basic human functioning capabilities. Once we reach the threshold of functioning, we have the real option of living our lives as we wish.

RIGHTS AND CAPABILITIES

Nussbaum argues that the capabilities approach is a better way to address injustices than is a rights-based approach. She gives three reasons for this. First, unlike capabilities, there are differing views on rights. That is, we agree on what capabilities people have. In the previous pages, we have reviewed many of the different ways that people can articulate rights and attendant obligations. On the other hand, regardless of what rights we believe people have, we might have different ideas about where rights come from. If we assume that rights are civil rights, then if a legitimate government does not allow freedom of religion or does not give a group of people the right to earn wages, there is no ground for challenging this government. The capabilities approach bypasses questions about what rights are and concentrates instead on what kind of beings we are and what it takes to have a flourishing human life. The second reason Nussbaum gives for the superiority of appealing to capabilities over rights to redress injustice is that to bring everyone to the functioning threshold of capabilities, we would have to treat people unequally. Under the capabilities approach, we are justified (and often required) to treat people unequally if that is necessary to bring everyone to a level where their capabilities can function. Rights, on the other hand, are typically understood to be justified claims that are held *equally* by all citizens.

According to the entitlement theory of rights, virtually all that is required of the government is to refrain from interfering in people's lives. The claims theory and wellbeing theory, on the other hand, both place obligations to others to uphold our rights. These theories are closer to my view. However, neither of them fully captures the importance that rights have in individuals' lives. Merely possessing rights is not enough to improve a person's quality of life. Rights theories do not obligate us to make sure these rights are actual options for people. The capabilities approach, on the other hand, not only demands that the government reflect these capabilities in its constitutional guarantees, but also ensures that everyone can enjoy them. As an example, in the United States, everyone has the right to get a higher education, and there are many government grants and opportunities for low-income students. However, going to college is not a realistic option for many poor students graduating from high school, because they do not know about these grants, they have not attended high schools that have prepared them for college, or simply because they have not been given the encouragement or the information that they need to consider college as a real option.

Third, as a pragmatic issue, rights are often viewed as a *western* idea, but capabilities are not. As mentioned in the previous chapter, critics of developing-world human rights violations are sometimes accused of being imperialists, often by leaders who are denounced for abusing their citizens. Capabilities talk, by contrast, might help us overcome the claims of imperialism by those who commit injustices. We can, perhaps, achieve more if we abandon talk of rights and speak instead of violation of capabilities. One reason for doing so is that it may be more inclusive of women as well as men because it averts discussion of women's rights, which can be a highly charged topic.

Nussbaum adopts the talk of rights only to justify the autonomy to choose which capabilities one will develop. But this ad hoc appeal is unnecessary. We have the capability to choose between our capabilities. This in itself can generate a right to do so. As for her pragmatic concern, we might wonder why this is particularly relevant in theoretical work. Moreover, the capabilities approach rests on empirical claims about human beings that are manifestly true in all cultures. If she is concerned with the pragmatic issue of using capability talk versus rights talk, she should avoid talk of rights here, too. It is pernicious here if it is pernicious anywhere. My view rids us of this ad hoc dichotomy of rights and capabilities by arguing that individuals' capabilities are the basis for their rights; the morally relevant capabilities generate corresponding rights and duties. Because capabilities existence is a universal empirical fact, we are engaging a universal human moral reality rather than confronting charges of western bias and cultural relativism.

In summary, the goals of public institutions should include the protection and promotion of the capabilities of each person, and they should "facilitate basic flourishing" (Khader 2011, 6). Such protection and promotion should be understood as a part of what justice requires. Nussbaum uses the capabilities approach as an alternative to rights talk. She argues that the language of capabilities is better than the language of rights to determine whether a government is oppressive. By contrast, I believe that capabilities generate rights. That is, if person x has the potential way of functioning y, then x must have the right to develop y as long as the development of y does not violate another's development of his or her capabilities. So, for instance, people have the right to political activism because they have the ability to participate in politics. However, not everyone will choose to be politically active. On the other hand, men would not have the right to receive an abortion because they do not have the potential way of functioning required for generating this right.

The capabilities approach as a basis for rights must respond to Nussbaum's concerns about using rights talk. Her first objection is that there are differing views on rights. The capabilities approach gets around the question of where rights come from. It gives us an understanding of rights as natural rights but avoids the major metaphysical and epistemological problems surrounding them. For instance, some theorists argue that natural rights are given by God, but in the capabilities view, rights are generated by each individual's capabilities—no deity needed. Human worth and dignity dictate that individuals have available to them a life worthy of humans, one that leads to human flourishing, if they are willing to take the opportunities life provides. People who are unable to acquire food are unable to live a flourishing life. Starving people cannot function in many ways. The same applies to those who are ill. In the capabilities view, because people have the capability of life and health, they have a right to access food and health care. Presumably, the securing of these rights will ultimately fall upon the government. Unfortunately, personal circumstances, such as unemployment or illness, do not eliminate one's right to life (such as food). Although we should not force adults to eat they ought to have access to food if they do choose to eat.

One might argue against the natural rights theory offered here and opt instead for civil rights theory. But the same epistemic issues appear here as well. We must ask what rights the legitimate government should grant its citizens and what kinds of rights we should agree on when we enter into a social contract. Capabilities-based rights solve these problems as well. In response to civil rights, we can argue that the government ought to grant rights that lead to human flourishing. If we base rights on capabilities, then we know what rights the government ought to support. In my reconstruction of the capabilities approach, in addition to Nussbaum's list of capabilities, there is always room for additional capabilities that she might have overlooked. It is imprudent to restrict our capabilities to our limited understanding of human nature.

The second reason Nussbaum gives for the superiority of capabilities over rights to address injustice is that, to bring everyone to the functioning threshold of capabilities, we would have to treat people unequally. According to Nussbaum, rights are held fully and equally by everyone, but capabilities require different levels of assistance to reach the threshold of functioning. Our commitment to justice, human flourishing, and human dignity obligates us to treat people differently to provide them with the opportunities to exercise their rights. Capabilities talk allows for these kinds of inequalities, so it is superior to rights talk. Nussbaum therefore recommends avoiding rights talk (except to address autonomy).

I agree with Nussbaum that some people require more than others to achieve the threshold of functioning. However, like capabilities, positive rights also generally require different levels of responses in different situations. My view entails that some people would have rights to more resources than others to achieve that threshold, not because they can afford more, but because they need more. According to Sen (1981, 11), rights are political goals. Governments should aim to achieve these goals (rights) for each individual. If we look at rights in this way, the capabilities approach will give us an accurate study of oppression in a particular society. We can assess how well each government ensures each person's development of capability and what rights are thereby granted to the citizens. If individuals who belong to a particular group are unable to get to the level of functioning and the government does not actively pursue that goal (which ensures their rights), there are grounds for concern that the government is oppressive.

Last, Nussbaum is concerned that rights are often taken to be a "western" idea, but capabilities do not have such a stigma. The issue here is that not all governments are receptive to rights language. Oppressive governments often assert their sovereignty to rule as they wish without intrusion from "western" ideals that, they claim, do not reflect the needs or the heritage of their countries or their citizens. If we start with capabilities talk instead of rights talk, we can accomplish more with those who do not welcome human rights discussions. Under the capabilities view, there is no dichotomy between rights and capabilities; we need not choose one over the other. After oppressive governments have accepted the language of capabilities and granted capabilities to their citizens, the move back to rights language is simple. This understanding of rights reframes them from a western idea to a human issue. The capabilities thus can provide a grounding theory for documents such as the United Nations' Universal Declaration of Human Rights. Once we recognize human capabilities, a list of rights is a short step away. For instance, if individuals, by virtue of being human, can psychologically flourish by having their capability of *Control Over One's Environment* developed through finding paid employment outside the house, then they ought to have the right to do so. Let's apply this idea to the Iranian American community.

THE IRANIAN AMERICAN COMMUNITY

It should be noted that in the United States, as well as in most capitalist societies, opportunities to develop our capabilities are often income-based. Those who live in poverty or lack resources for social mobility typically do not think they can make significant changes to their socioeconomic status. To some extent, they are right; society is structured so that not everyone has the same opportunities to develop their capabilities and to live according to their conception of the good. This is why I do not approve of looking at GNP or the aggregate good (utility) to decide whether a government has secured the means necessary for its citizens to develop their capabilities. The aggregate might appear promising even when resources are distributed unjustly and some individuals' capabilities are obstructed. For instance, aggregated figures suggest a misleading portrait of Iranian Americans. According to a study conducted at MIT, Iranian Americans are the most highly educated ethnic group in the United States . . . [and] hold five times the number of doctorates than the national average . . . . The per capita average income of Iranian-Americans is 50% higher than that of the nation, while family average income is 38% higher. The percentage of Iranian-Americans living in homes valued more than $1 million is nearly 10 times that of the national average. (Mostashari and Khodamhosseini 2004, 1–2)

However, this apparent socioeconomic success does not immunize our community against oppression and mistreatment. As the African American community has discovered to its dismay, regardless of how we act, and no matter our socioeconomic status, income, or education, our community experiences hostility and racism both socially and legally (King and Wheelock 2007).

Iranian Americans are systematically targeted because of our group membership and the negative stereotypes about our community. Oppression occurs because we are racialized as "not-white" in one way or another—as "Middle Eastern," "Arab," "Asian," "Brown," "Black," or "foreign." Iranian people immigrate to the United States for a better life, one free of oppression and free from fear of the government's unmistakably inhuman treatment of its population. We seek an escape from the lack of jobs and educational opportunities, and from the authoritarian Islamic government with its climate of censorship. Yet as we leave that stifling climate behind, we find ourselves victimized by racist people who perceive us as dangerous. We exchange one kind of oppression for another. We give up our home, family, friends, and some of us our jobs, for freedom in the United States, but still we find ourselves chained by oppression.

According to the capabilities approach, we must not destroy a basic human capability in exchange for social gains for either individuals or society. Basic capabilities and social gains are different kinds of goods; they are radically unalike in nature. Iranian American immigrants navigate this space by giving up some capabilities for others. We fear violation of bodily integrity and emotional wellbeing, so we shy away from social and political involvement, which entail the development of capabilities that relate to one's public life. Those of us who are least assimilated into American culture tend to feel unwelcome and unappreciated, so we trade our social and political affiliations, the activities that provide self-actualization beyond the family and home environment, for safety. Being disconnected from such activities fulfills the definition of oppression: "being cut off from the sorts of activities that define what it is to be human" (Bartky 1990, 31). Feeling vulnerable, many Iranian women who immigrate with their spouses choose to be homemakers and full-time mothers especially if they are not proficient in English, which in many cases systematically and unjustly disengages them from public life, violating their capability to be involved in the public realm and gain economic freedom. Some do not have the resources—education, job skills, self-confidence, or language skills—to change their lives. If a person must trade a social good in order to have safety, food, or health care (basic capabilities), we have reason to suspect that the situation is oppressive.

The capabilities theory of rights fits well in our analysis here. *Prima facie* it seems unreasonable to claim that people should have the right to emotional health and that the government is somehow responsible for providing or ensuring it. However, when we consider that the trauma of having one's emotional wellbeing violated can affect all aspects of a person's life, it appears more reasonable to claim a right to emotional health. Feminist economist Julie A. Nelson (2004) draws from the capabilities approach to show the importance of emotions in the realm of economic development. One of the best known to Americans is the use of advertising, which often appeals to our emotions, to sell things. She further points to reproductive labor, and caring labor, and the fact that these kinds of unpaid work demand emotional interdependence which often goes ignored. Although the discussion of emotions, and acting from emotions have been historically frowned upon in western philosophy as well as in the studying of economics, Nelson reminds us that,

> Emotion both informs and motivates people. Feelings of fear or joy give us important information about our environment. People act, not just because they 'have reason to', but also from their gut, because they 'feel moved'. Feelings, desires, urges, motivations, reactions, sentiments—whatever we call them—are part of human life. Emotions are what make us desire freedom, or desire the use of reason. (314)

We would be mistaken to deny the effects of emotions in the decisions that we make. Additionally, being emotionally, socially and individually grounded, and having a solid sense of self requires some level of connectedness with others. Ignoring the capability of emotion (by economists or others) is unwise, and gives us an incomplete understanding for analysis and theory development. The capability of emotion is "co-equal" with the capability of reason and plays an important role in identity and economic development (320).

The government's commitment to ensure that the capability of emotions can achieve the threshold of functioning is limited by biological factors such as chemical imbalances in the brain. However, there are structures that the governments can put in place to support metal health. Access to health care is essential to this aim, because that could address both the physiological as well as the psychological needs of individuals. Prevalence of mental health is different in different groups. Those who struggle with some kind of socially induced disadvantages might struggle more with metal health issues. Racial minorities report significantly more emotional challenges than their white counterparts (Martinez and Graham-LoPresti, 2018). The Iranian Americans who have also experienced war and violence, in addition to overt racism or micro-aggressions, find themselves in a significantly challenging situation. As I have mentioned before, governments can't address every single situation that affects individuals' mental health state but there are steps to be taken that benefit both the individual and the society. The 2018 Global Happiness Policy Report states that "each dollar of mental health expenditure leads to an extra 2.5 dollars of GDP, made possible by expanded employment of those with improved metal health" (Helliwell 2018, 15). The Mental Health Foundation of London, England, recommends that we address five priorities that address inequalities in a holistic way. They are: healthy children, healthy mind, healthy places, healthy communities, and healthy habits (Health Inequalities Manifesto, 2018). Healthy mind is our focus here, but that is a collection of steps that leads to one's emotional wellbeing.

The capabilities approach is a useful tool for analyzing and correcting social and political inequalities. Evaluating the community's opportunities for development is essential in deciding what resources are needed to create a socially just society, "taking into account social and institutional structures as conversion factors which demand equality interventions" (Loots and Walker 2016, 262). The conversion factors that Loots and Walker refer to are the individual factors, as well as interpersonal comparison, in their case between the genders within a society, and how they interact with social institutions. When a government grants its citizens legal rights but social justice is lacking, or when legal rights are not granted, the capabilities approach can give guidelines for how citizens should proceed if they wish to establish their rights. Loots and Walker distinguish between the evaluative and prospective applications of the capabilities approach: "an evaluative analysis focuses on *which* capabilities are expanded, for *whom* and to *what extent.* Whereas with prospective analysis, the focus moves towards *how* and *why* capabilities are expanded" (263). They add that policy development would start with the evaluative process and then "identify which concrete actions are likely to generate a great stream of expanded capabilities," which is the role of the prospective application of capabilities (263).

Almost everyone agrees that no one should be unjustly harmed, but we do not all agree on what constitutes harm or justice. I hold that "harm" is any unjustified violation of capabilities. I agree with Nussbaum that basic human capabilities are necessary for flourishing human life. If opportunity to develop these capabilities is taken away from a person, their potential for a good life is decreased. For example, if my capability of *Play* is taken away, I lose a huge joy in my life. Lack of play has been connected to many psychological disorders, which we can agree detracts from a flourishing life. Those in the Iranian

American community, along with others who fear for their safety, have their capability of *Play* significantly thwarted. Other non-basic capabilities might be significant in recognizing and addressing other inequalities in society, or they may have "instrumental significance" for other capabilities (Burchardt and Hick 2018, 43). One might not care about their neighbor's mental health or if they are happy, but they care about the unemployment rate. One could argue that addressing mental health in the community would decrease the unemployment rate. In that case, we are better off addressing issues that take away one's capability of *Play* that might cause mental health issues. Although seemingly a minor issue, together small instances would create a web of oppression. So, when a particular group of people, such as Iranian Americans, lacks one or more of the non-basic capabilities, we should suspect that their situation is oppressive.

CHAPTER SUMMARY

The capabilities-based approach to rights provides a better way than the traditional understanding of rights to assess whether a society or its institutions are oppressive based on the society's own standards. Rights should be the goal of, rather than the basis for, a society. Capabilities are a better way to start. Governments should be evaluated on what rights they are able to guarantee and protect. If a government does not have the means to provide a particular good (e.g., an education past high school), then its citizens are not oppressed by their lack of education, although they may be poor. Oppression is a particular kind of harm; not all harms are instances of oppression, only those that violate one's capabilities. The citizens may still be entitled to assistance from outside, but not because people are oppressed. However, the citizens count as oppressed if their government has the means to provide higher education but chooses not to do so.

A capabilities-based theory of rights is a version of natural rights that circumvents some of the issues related to traditional views of natural rights and avoids other difficulties associated with the three theories of rights that I have discussed in this chapter: rights as entitlements, rights as claims, and rights as wellbeing. The capabilities approach answers the objections against each. In this chapter, I have expressed certain commitments to justice, such as equal opportunity for exercising one's rights, and the only construction that can keep those commitments is the capabilities theory of rights.

Chapter Five

Harms of Oppression

RACE AND PASSING

In the previous chapters, I have discussed oppression, the capabilities approach, rights, and race. In this chapter, I will use the theoretical framework established in the previous chapters to discuss racial oppression (racism) and make suggestions on how to end it. Specifically, I will discuss the harms typical of racial oppression and propose measures to counter them, some of which go beyond the construct of rights. My discussion will address the ways that people who are passing are, and are not, oppressed. I will argue that these people benefit by passing, yet still are victims of racial oppression, although the victimization is generally internally inflicted. The internalization of stereotypes is due to society-wide negative stereotypes.

Racial oppression is not merely morally wrong. The American Academy of Pediatrics recently published a policy statement outlining the "profound impact [of racism] on the health status of children, adolescents, emerging adults, and their families" (Trent, Dooley, and Douge 2019, 2). Maria Trent, Danielle Dooley, and Jacqueline Douge refer to racism as a "socially transmitted disease passed down through generations, leading to inequalities observed in our population today" (3). Those who experience racism and the stresses it causes suffer from mental health issues, bodily inflammation leading to chronic illnesses, low infant birth weight, and other adverse health outcomes. Racism's effects are also observed in the juvenile justice system, schools, the workplace, health-care settings, financial systems, and most other social institutions. Each encounter with racism has a cumulative negative effect that violates the capabilities of life, bodily integrity, health, joy, friendship, and political affiliation. This fundamentally damages the human experiences of those who experience racial oppression.

Racism's harms are inflicted because of one's racialization. In chapter 2, I proposed a definition of race that I will use in this chapter to discuss the effect of oppression's harms on individuals of a particular race, regardless of whether they are racialized as part of that group or pass as white. A group is racialized if

1. Individuals in the group are socially positioned as subordinate or privileged along some dimension (economic, political, legal, social, etc.), because
2. The group satisfies "the criteria central to the application of a folk racial concept" (Mallon 2004, 661) and
3. The individuals within the group occupy a location (a society, culture, or group) within which race is used to divide people.

This view of race accounts for the notion that those who pass as white experience racial oppression because the folk theory in the United States typically holds that if a person has ancestry from a particular geographic location, they are part of the racial group that stems from that region. According to the folk theory of race, if someone *looks* Black, they *are* Black, even if they do not identify as Black. For example, a dark-skinned Iranian American typically suffers the same disadvantages in the United States as Black people do. On the other hand, consider a person who has a Black ancestor but who looks white and is white-passing. They are not racialized as white, so they benefit socially from their appearance and racialization, even though they might also suffer some harms of oppression.

TYPICAL HARMS OF RACIAL OPPRESSION

The normative criterion of oppression is harm, which is the violation of one's capabilities. I will discuss six harms of racial oppression, some of which I have already touched on in the previous chapters: violence, economic deprivation, moral exclusion, cultural imperialism, a sense of injustice, and the harmful consequences of stereotyping. These harms are not self-imposed, and they are inflicted due to a person's membership in a particular racial group. Group membership can be voluntary or involuntary: "members of voluntary social groups share joint commitments or joint projects. The members of a non-voluntary social group share social penalties and rewards consequent on their being so grouped" (Cudd 2006, 41). Members of a racial group do not necessarily share a project, history, or religion. They instead are bound by their common oppression or common benefits gained from the membership in that group, and by how society typically racializes their group's members.

Sometimes we are racially categorized into a group that we might not identify with. For instance, in south Texas, I lived in a community that often classified me as Mexican American. In my view, Mexican American is not only a nationality or ethnicity but also a race because it entails disadvantage, and because the term "Mexican American" is currently used in the United States to refer to a race. Moreover, we treat Mexican Americans more like African Americans (a racial group) than like Irish Americans (an ethnic group); race is a category of disadvantage or privilege, whereas ethnicity does not connote hierarchy. Mexican whites are not classified as racially white in our society, although this might change at some point in the future. Additionally, as mentioned before, race does not travel. One can be racialized one way in one society and differently in another society. For instance, a woman from Senegal once told me that, in Senegal, I would be classified as white, but with my Iranian background, dark brown eyes, and black hair, I am not likely to be racialized in the United States as white.

Because we live in a highly racialized society, being racially categorized has both benefits and penalties—some racial categorizations are beneficial and others are harmful. The oppressed (those who are marginalized) face harmful situations financially, emotionally, and physically. These are not mutually exclusive categories: The physical harms cause emotional ones, emotional harms cause physical harms, and both can affect one's financial status. Each of these harms can be either externally (involuntarily) or internally (voluntarily) inflicted, but the voluntary infliction of harm on oneself is the most insidious case of oppression and the most difficult to detect and fight against.

Violence

In chapter 3, I discussed Iris Young's five faces of oppression, one of which is violence. Victims of violence "suffer the oppression of systematic and legitimate violence. The members of some groups live with the knowledge that they must fear random, unprovoked attacks on their persons or property, which have no motive but to damage, humiliate, or destroy the person" (Young 1988, 287). The examples of violence are numerous in marginalized populations, but my focus is on the Iranian American community, which experiences unprovoked violence, humiliation, and ongoing racism and discrimination. The two recent murders of Iranian American men, one at the hands of a white supremacist (Emery 2019), and the other by a police officer (Jackman 2019), recall the alarming trend that the African American community has faced.

Some of this violence stems from the contentious relationship between the governments of Iran and the United States (White 1970). Negative messages about Iran and Iranians as hostile, angry, West-hating, and uncompromising continue to appear in the media and affect how (non-Iranian) Americans feel about their Iranian American fellow citizens. Those who work in jobs stereotypically held by Middle Easterners (taxi drivers, convenience store owners, hotel owners) are more likely to experience hate crimes than are those who do not (Paige, Hatfield, and Liang 2015). Iranian American Muslim men are more likely to experience harassment than are either Iranian American Muslim women or Iranian Americans who belong to other religious groups.

Harassment, a form of non-physical violence, faced by Iranian Americans is both political and personal, as I mentioned in chapter 1. Shari Paige, Elaine Hatfield, and Lu Liang give us a summary to illustrate the political harassment that the community has experienced in the past few years.

> [C]onservative commentator Ann Coulter referred to Iranians as "ragheads." Brent Scowcroft, a one-time National Security Agency advisor, called the Iranian people "rug merchants." The *Columbus Dispatch* recently ran a cartoon portraying Iran as a sewer with cockroaches crawling out of it. Debra Cagan, a senior official at the Pentagon, declared: "I hate all Iranians." In March, 2015, John Bolton, one-time U.S. ambassador to the United Nations, in a *New York Times* op-ed piece, advised, "To Stop Iran's Bomb, Bomb Iran." (2015, 237)

These are just examples of the dehumanizing images of Iranians and Iranian Americans that taint the common perception of the Iranian American community. These clear cases of violence, both physical and verbal, are inflicted externally. Resisting these kinds of harms is futile and perhaps impossible. But other harms of oppression are more subtle; they are integrated into the institutional racism of our social structure.

Economic Deprivation

One of the main components of the Civil Rights Act of 1964 was to prohibit employment discrimination based on race and sex. But even though laws now ban employment discrimination, they do not protect everyone at all times. During and after the hostage crisis of 1979–1981, the Iranian American community faced just such a situation. Iranian Americans who had just started looking for work in the late 1970s and early 1980s struggled to find jobs after completing their education. In her memoir, *Funny in Farsi,* Firoozeh Dumas (2004) recounts that her father, after earning an engineering degree in the United States in the 1970s, encountered many obstacles in finding a job and eventually moved back to Iran. Mohsen Mobasher (2012) and Neda Maghbouleh (2017) also give detailed accounts of Iranian Americans' experiences during that time, some of which I have discussed in previous chapters.

To make matters worse, some of those who had earned college degrees in the United States and were looking for jobs could not return to Iran. Some were anti-revolutionaries, and others faced being drafted to fight in a war they did not support between Iran and Iraq. Those with student visas were forbidden to work. Some relied on their families for funding, but many families lost their wealth. Others depended financially on scholarships from the Iranian government or Iranian universities; these sources of income, too, disappeared suddenly. Therefore, many Iranians living in the United States were in legal limbo, leaving their lives economically, socially, and politically unstable. Their financial situation was dire, and, given their accent, appearance, and socioeconomic status, they were more likely to face discrimination than were those in wealthier homes (Paige, Hatfield, and Liang 2015, 24).

Despite these challenges, the Iranian American community has mostly recovered. As discussed in chapter 1, Iranian Americans' household income is higher than the U.S. average. Iran's so-called "brain drain," which began after the 1979 revolution, continues; the country sends its most promising students and professionals abroad, along with their wealth (Torbat 2002; Krever 2017). Iranian culture, which places high regard on education, hard work, and prosperity, continues to thrive in the United States. However, the current U.S. sanctions on Iran have cut off the Iranian American community from opportunities both in Iran and abroad. Iranians who once did business in Iran, trading in rugs, art, or food, are no longer allowed to continue these commercial exchanges. A handful of Caribbean islands have banned *all* Iranians, including those who live in the United States, from investing in businesses in their country (St. Aimee 2018). Since 2012, Iranians in good legal standing in the United States, Canada, and Great Britain have found their bank accounts frozen simply because they are Iranians, on the assumption that these accounts are tied to the Iranian government (Hembree 2018). Lack of access to one's earnings violates one's civil rights and liberties. Payment companies, such as Venmo and PayPal, have begun flagging any transaction with the words "Iranian" or "Persian" in them. "Friends transferring money to one another to pay for food at a Persian restaurant are flagged and scrutinized, while transactions with words like Heil Hitler, Nazis, KKK, cocaine, and heroin—all of which go against Venmo and Paypal's policies—are not flagged or blocked" (Ghandehari 2019, para. 6). The National Iranian American Council reports that Iranian Americans also currently face employment difficulties. Its website highlights the case of Sahar Nowruzzadeh, who was demoted from her position in the State Department due to her ethnic origin—she was born in the United States—and an investigation concluded that she was indeed a victim of discrimination (Abdi 2019, para. 4). These are just some examples of economic obstacles faced by Iranian Americans in the United States.

Moral Exclusion

Moral exclusion refers to "the limited applicability of justice underlying destructive conflicts and difficult social problems" (Opotow, Gerson, and Woodside 2005, 303). Having a restricted *scope of justice,* "the psychological boundary within which concerns about fairness govern our conduct," sets up those on the outside as beyond our moral consideration. It sets up people who are morally "not considered" for "deprivation, exploitation, and other harms that might be ignored or condoned as normal, inevitable, and deserved" (305). Individuals and groups outside of moral inclusion find themselves targeted by rudeness, intimidation, hate crimes, and violence against their person or properties, as well as elements of structural racism such as poverty, cultural imperialism, mass murder, and other grave violations of human rights. "*Moral inclusion* captures the dynamics of peace building in its emphasis on fairness, source sharing, and concern for the well-being of all" (Opotow, Gerson and Woodside 2005, 304).

According to Mark Bernstein (1998, 9), people have moral considerability because they have the "capacity to absorb moral consideration." Although Bernstein agrees that we "ought" to morally consider agents who possess moral considerability, he makes a distinction between the normative and descriptive sense of moral considerability, and holds that he uses the term descriptively. Additionally, Kenneth Goodpaster (1978) distinguishes between having the capacity of moral considerability and having moral rights. One might possess one and not the other. In the view that I proposed in chapter 4 on the capabilities approach, the person who has the capacity to be considered morally has the moral right to be considered in the moral community. Hence, their exclusion is immoral and unjust. If this exclusion happens in a systemic way to a group of people because of their group membership, we would have good reason to think it constitutes oppression.

The exclusion can be subtle or blatant, dehumanizing, and psychologically hurtful. Morton Deutsch (2011, 110) asks us to consider whether there are differences in how people are treated, whether "some people [are] apt to lose their jobs, be excluded from obtaining scarce resources, or be scapegoated and victimized." In the sections above, I have gathered examples showing how the Iranian American community has been excluded from moral consideration. Moral inclusivity requires that we consider everyone's wellbeing, but that has not been the case with the Iranian American community. We have been morally excluded; we fear harassment, violence, disrespect, job instability, and racist neighbors, students, teachers, bankers, and grocery store clerks. Moral exclusion leaves us socially and politically isolated, which is emotionally distressing and self-limiting. Although moral exclusion can lead to physical violence and even genocide, it also thwarts the development of capabilities that we use in social aspects of life: emotions, affiliation, other species, play, and control over one's political and material environment.

Cultural Imperialism

One of the harms of oppression, discussed in chapter 3, is cultural imperialism, which "consists in the universalization of one group's experience and culture, and its establishment as the norm" (Young 1988, 285). The marginalized group, in our case the Iranian American community, responds in one of two ways: either we assimilate as much as we can into the non-Iranian community, or we maintain our subculture and socialize mostly with Iranian Americans. Those gatherings are generally not visible to the dominant group. This kind of separation of cultures causes division, but private space is also a safer place for marginalized populations. These are spaces where we can be ourselves, where we do not have to explain ourselves or our behavior, food, culture, or language. In other words, we do not have to be emotionally on guard in such spaces.

It is true that most people have a public and a private persona. We wear different hats and play different roles in different situations. However, being "ourselves" refers to something different in addition to this: "Culturally dominated groups often experience themselves as having a double identity, one defined by the dominant group and the other coming from membership in one's own group" (Deutsch 2011, 106). In the dominant culture, marginalized populations might be the victims of harassment. One's immigration status, language abilities, level of cultural assimilation, and appearance all play a role in how we are treated. A person might have held a prestigious position in Iran as a doctor, engineer, or business owner, or might be a respected elder in one's community, but in the United States they might be working as a cab driver, grocery store clerk, janitor, or even be jobless due to their inability to speak proper English. A wise person once said, "just because I speak with an accent doesn't mean I think with one." Regardless of one's abilities and education, having an accent often means being treated as though one is uneducated, illiterate, even mentally challenged. One's accomplishments and identities might lead to respect in one's home culture but disparagement and disrespect in the dominant culture.

Sense of Injustice

Deutsch points out that having a sense of injustice can be a harm of oppression. A sense of injustice refers to one's ability to recognize injustice when it occurs. Awareness of one's own oppression causes anger, humiliation, resentment, depression, and helplessness regarding the prospect of the situation's improvement. Not everyone is equally aware of the injustices around them or those inflicted on them: "Whether an injustice takes the form of physical abuse, discrimination in employment, sexual harassment, or disrespectful treatment, there will always be some people who are insensitive to the injustice and hence seemingly unaware of it" (Deutsch 2011, 100). Being aware of one's role in oppressing others causes guilt and fear of revenge. Generally, the oppressor is in a position of privilege and power, and they aim to diffuse responsibility. In some cases, victims are told that they are unfounded in their recognition of the experience as oppressive. This may take the form of *gaslighting*. Gaslighting refers to (1) a person manipulating another person to believe something false about themselves, as in the case of the 1938 Patrick Hamilton play and 1944 film, *Gaslight*. In the movie the husband has his wife hospitalized by convincing her that she is mentally unstable; and (2) a person does not believe one's testimony of their experience. The latter is our interest here. Gaslighting is a phenomenon that,

> . . . a hearer doesn't believe, or expresses doubt about, a speaker's testimony. . . . the hearer of testimony raises doubts about the speaker's reliability at perceiving events accurately. Directly, or indirectly, then, gaslighting involves expressing doubts that the harm or injustice that the speaker is testifying to really happened as the speaker claims. (McKinnon 2017, 168)

Gaslighting is not always intentional, but it is always hurtful. It sends the message to the victim that their sense of reality monitoring is flawed and that their experience of injustice did not happen. If the speaker's credibility is constantly undermined, our epistemic agency is thwarted. This is a form of what Miranda Fricker (2007, 20) refers to as epistemic injustice, as it discounts one of the most central aspects of being a person: being a knower. Gaslighting can also stem from the hearer's stereotypes about a speaker. These stereotypes can result in the speaker being assigned *Credibility Deficit* (Fricker 2007, 17). This deficit could be assigned due to one's gender, race, class, accent, political affiliation, and so on. So, as Rachel McKinnon points out, "testimonial injustice disrespects people qua persons" (McKinnon 2017, 168). The capabilities approach can detect these harms as immoral and as the basis of oppression. Fricker also agrees that something "ethically bad" has happened here, which takes the form of epistemic injustice. Our relations with others depend on whether we can trust them and whether they are able to acknowledge our agency. When gaslighting occurs, it makes one question one's sense of justice and doubt one's own experiences. This is a common experience among marginalized populations. It affects our sense of trust, our connections with other people, and causes anger and resentment at having our experiences denied and questioned.

Stereotyping

In the first chapter, I introduced the notion of stereotyping; here, I will build a bit on that structure. Research shows that stereotyping a group has a vast impact on the way the individuals within the group understand themselves. Katherine Reynolds et al. (2000, 276) found that "stereotyping emerged as a fairly unambiguously negative force within social relations characterized by power differentials—it contributes to control, constraint, distortion, domination and false consciousness." This control is not physical; it is implanted in the minds of the people who are stereotyped. They add that "Those with power can control ideas, beliefs, and stereotypes in the same way they control other social and material resources and can thereby instill a 'false consciousness' in the powerless such that the powerless become complicit in their own disadvantage." The powerless accept their own oppression and become their own oppressors: "It is not that they [the psychologically oppressed] will prefer oppression to justice, or subordination to equality, rather they will prefer the kinds of social roles that tend to subordinate them, make them less able to choose, or give them fewer choices to make" (Cudd 2006, 181). Those are the roles typically expected of them. Those who are negatively stereotyped in society internalize the stereotypes, and the resulting negative mindset becomes a limiting factor in the ways they conduct their lives.

Just about every group suffers or benefits from social stereotypes. These harms and benefits are multi-dimensional. Consider the stereotypes in the United States describing Iranian Americans as being aggressive, anti-West, suspicious, and hostile (Paige, Hatfield, and Liang 2015). These stereotypes, as psychologists have shown, negatively affect our perceptions of ourselves and our roles in society. The development of race is a social phenomenon. We learn about race, racial identity, and stereotypes about race by being in society and through relations to other people. So, our racialization is also a social process.

According to research done by Reynolds et al. (2000), stereotyping is a social phenomenon that leads to self-stereotyping. We internalize stereotypes (social expectations of us) and act accordingly. Society-wide stereotypes are a huge determining factor in what one would expect of one's life prospects. Hence, we become voluntary victims of oppression through self-stereotyping. These harms are seen as an extension of who people are and not of the social structure that has made their world such that they are forced to adopt the preferences that they have.

Stereotyping affects groups in different ways. Judith Howard (1984) points out that stereotypes also affect the way we react to the misfortunes of some groups that are negatively stereotyped. "Stereotypes influence our reaction to members of these groups. Those who subscribe to the stereotypes of young black men as aggressive and hostile, for example, may attribute the unemployment of a particular young black man to his presumed hostile disposition, ignoring current economic circumstances" (Howard 1984, 271). Consequently, we see no reason to address the institutional oppression that Black people face, but rather we blame them for supposedly having a violent culture, which is in opposition to the "civilized and calm" European one. I often experience these kinds of sentiments about Iranian Americans as well. We blame the victims for their victimization by questioning their demeanor, interview skills, language use, and so on, but not the possibility of their being victims of racism.

These three harms of oppression are not necessarily mutually exclusive, as we have seen in the examples given in the two sections above. Each could happen by itself or be the result of another harm. For instance, violence and economic oppression could lead to self-stereotyping. Self-stereotyping has grave consequences for one's life and limits one's choices. Regardless of whether a person's racial identity is apparent to society—whether a person is passing or not—they can be victims of self-stereotyping.

HARMS OF OPPRESSION: PASSING (OR NOT)

In chapter 1, I discussed Iranian Americans who pass as white. People who are passing and those who are close to them face emotional challenges in response to their passing. These challenges, although personal, have political, social, and personal implications. A passing person might "racially" identify with the original designation of their group, but they could be mistaken; their identification, as I have argued in chapter 2, is ethnic identity. If I pass as Mexican in my racialization and live my life accordingly, then I am no longer (publicly) living as Iranian American. If I suffer the harms that the Mexican American community does, then my racialization is Mexican American. However, I might identify with the Hispanic race, but I do not ethnically belong to that group, since I am culturally (or ethnically) Iranian American. Many Iranians living in the Rio Grande Valley in South Texas speak Spanish, are married to Mexicans, eat mostly Mexican foods, celebrate Mexican holidays, and seem to be a better fit with the Mexican American than the Iranian American community. Although they pass as Mexicans, they identify ethnically as Iranians or Persians.

Because most of the racialization of people is done in order to classify, categorize, or stereotype them, the negative or positive stereotypes will affect them whether they are passing or not. If someone identifies with the oppressed race, whether or not they are passing, this identification can and often does lead to voluntary oppression. Those who are passing could be victims of psychological oppression due to stereotyping, the traditional understanding of race, and their own racial or ethnic identification. They are not victims of external forces of oppression; rather, they internalize society's *traditional* categorization of their "race," and the stereotypes that go along with it. The psychologically oppressed internalize the traditional understanding of race along with all the historical and current negative stereotypes that go along with it, and become their own oppressors.

Kwame Anthony Appiah (1990, 498) reminds us of those who disagree with the practice of passing altogether and consider it to be a moral offense. Piper (1992) also shares her struggle with passing people. Adrian Piper's personal challenges in dealing with passing people resonate with me, but I do not agree with Appiah's view that passing is immoral. Race is an evolving concept. We are *racialized* in society. It is not possible to determine a person's race by appealing to certain essential characteristics. Likewise, a person's race does not determine any facts about their abilities. Therefore, it is not important whether a person identifies with the race to which they "belong." So, there is no moral offense in being racialized one way or another. In my view of race, no one is really passing. People belong to the race that they are racialized to by others. Some Iranian Americans do not identify with their racialization as Iranian Americans, even though they might like the food, speak the language, and sometimes celebrate traditional holidays. These people are passing, but society is always going to racialize them as other, even though they do not identify with that racialization.

We live in a society where race matters a great deal. As Charles Mills (1998, 43) notes, we have a vertical (in contrast to horizontal) race system in the United States: "one's racial designation will have immense significance, since it will indicate one's social standing and profoundly affect one's life." That is, there is a close correlation between race and socioeconomic status. In such a society, it is rational to hide one's race if it works against one's social status. In a society where race works on a horizontal system, which "race has no present or historical link with political power, economic wealth, cultural influence: the races are randomly distributed in the social order" (43). We don't live in a horizontal system of race. If one is racialized as Iranian American and Iranian Americans are discriminated against, it is beneficial to hide one's racial identity. However, passing people who internalize their social designation and the negative stereotypes about their group may become victims of self-stereotyping while still also suffering externally from the negative stereotypes.

According to Claudia Steele and Joshua Aronson (1995), widespread negative stereotypes against one's group lead to stereotype threat, which refers to one's awareness or suspicion that others are constantly watching and judging, looking for evidence that one conforms to stereotypes about one's group. Steele and Aronson (1995, 797) contend that "the existence of such stereotypes means that anything one does or any of one's features that conform to it make the stereotype more plausible as a self-characterization in the eyes of others, and perhaps even in one's own eyes." Black and Brown people often feel that they live under a microscope, as if the whole of society is watching. Even the most miniscule acts that correspond to the stereotypes serve to propagate the negative stereotypes against us, keeping us in a socially inferior situation.

Those who are passing are subject to self-shame as well as stereotype threat. Internalizing our inferior social status, we feel ashamed to be the kind of person described by the stereotypes. When my daughter, who looks white, was born, an Iranian American family member told me I should be glad my daughter is white because white children are smarter and more polite than non-white children. This individual is not white, nor am I, so her statement is pregnant with self-shame. According to Sandra Bartky (1990, 30), "many oppressed persons come to regard themselves as uniquely unable to satisfy normal criteria of psychological health or moral adequacy. To believe that my inferiority is a function of the kind of person I am may make me ashamed of being of *this* kind." Self-shame is insidious. By leading one to low self-esteem, self-shame limits one's development of capabilities and thereby perpetuates stereotypes.

Both self-shame and stereotype threat have damaging consequences. First, they are limiting. They thwart the development of one's capabilities and aim to mold people's lives into patterns that might not suit them. Second, stereotype threat can lead to what Steele and Aronson (1995, 798) call "immediate situational threat," which is the risk of being judged and treated stereotypically. Due to immediate situational threat, some people who are members of oppressed groups but who are in positions of relative privilege will refuse to help the less privileged members of their group. Stereotype threat

> can befall anyone with a group identity about which some negative stereotype exists, and for the person to be threatened in this way he need not even believe the stereotype. He need only know that it stands as a hypothesis about him in situations where the stereotype is relevant. (Steele and Aronson 1995, 798)

Research shows that stereotype threat and immediate situational threat both can (and often do) result in poor performance on intellectual tests. Stereotype threat and situational threat work differently in different people. People may internalize inferiority, or they may blame others for their problems and "underutilized available opportunities," but both responses contribute to their second-class status (Steele and Aronson 1995, 798). For instance, self-blame can lead people to see themselves as lacking the capability to succeed, causing them not to put forth much effort. I suppose we all suffer from this to some extent. As an example, I have always wanted to be a good painter, but I do not believe that I have the talent for it and have never tried (and never will). However, this does not hinder my life options or my quality of life, nor does it leave me in an oppressed social status. But consider a different situation: A young Black man has internalized negative stereotypes and therefore believes he will not succeed in college, so he does not even apply for admission. Because he believes his lack of higher education is due to his own inabilities, he is unlikely to recognize and resist the structural, systemic racism that prevents Black men from succeeding in college. Self-blame is thus the final and key element that perpetuates oppression.

On the other hand, blaming others can also lead one to avoid taking chances, because one might believe that others will always prevent one from succeeding. Therefore, one would "underutilize" the available resources that would help one succeed. In this way, blaming others can have the same result as self-blame: both can end in situations that diminish one's abilities and, consequently, lower one's quality of life. In the next chapter, I will discuss some ways to address oppression.

Chapter Six

Responding to Oppression

FORCES THAT KEEP OPPRESSION IN PLACE

To overcome oppression, we need to understand what perpetuates it. Some of the forces are more obvious, such as the fact that those in positions of power create and enforce laws that are beneficial to themselves. Additionally, it's typically white people who have "[c]ontrol over the institutions (such as the family, school, church, and media) which socialize and indoctrinate people to accept the power inequalities; and interactive power in which there are repeated individual behaviors by those who are more powerful which confirm the subordinate status of those in low power" (Deutsch 2011, 202). Government officials can also continue the oppression of a group by sanctioned violence against them, or by "unofficial terror," which is "perpetuated by private individuals from dominant groups, often illegally, with the tacit approval of public officials (as in the lynching of African-American men accused of having sex with white women" (Deutsch 2011, 202). Although Iranian Americans are not being lynched in the United States, *unofficial terrors* continue, such as the isolation and discrimination that Iranian Americans experience in society. Control over socialization and indoctrination by educational institutions, churches, mass media, friends, and family are other factors that perpetuate oppressive practices. These indoctrinations situate both the oppressor and the oppressed to have certain expectations and fill different roles.

HOW TO ADDRESS OPPRESSION?

The U.S. government keeps introducing new programs to help people of color. However, these often address the symptoms of oppression rather than the oppressive social structures themselves. According to Sandra Van Dyke (1993, 82–83), if we understand race theory and race within the social and historical perspective of the United States, we will recognize that government "action . . . has sapped valuable energies and resources [by] working on fruitless programs." It is important to view the racial situation from an institutional perspective. Van Dyke adds that

> Little, if any, money is spent by public or private agencies for economic development to create infrastructures within African [American] communities that would be self-sustaining and would allow for community development. Because of their deleterious effects on African [American] people, culturally, politically, and economically these theories cannot offer any viable hope for liberation from the constant and continuing pressures of a racist society. (83)

This is the injustice of racial oppression in the United States. All individuals living within a society ought to have the means required to achieve the threshold of functioning. In my view, people possess not only negative rights but also positive rights to some opportunities. This implies, for instance, that opening universities' doors to racial minorities might not be sufficient to help them view college as a real option. In other words, society must provide them the means to progress to the point that they realize they are capable of making a better life for themselves. Education is one way to do so.

Rights

Each individual has the right to live in a society that does not degrade or humiliate them. Social justice demands that one not be made ashamed of one's race, suffer the threat of stereotypes, or be intellectually degraded. Stereotype threat and self-shame thwart individuals' abilities to develop capabilities; in the view that I have proposed, this constitutes the violation of one's rights.

In chapter 4, I argued for a capabilities-based theory of rights. Violation of one's development of capabilities is the violation of one's rights. Negative self-stereotyping can and often does lead people to avoid attempting to develop their capabilities. One can have one's rights violated (capabilities destroyed) not only by physical force, but also by years of socialization. Stereotyping, poor education, and lack of health care or other services all lead individuals to develop negative self-images. As I mentioned earlier, this is oppressive.

Stereotyping violates individuals' rights by preventing them from developing their capabilities. For instance, if we have the capability of having control over our political environment—which virtually all people do—then we ought to have the right to effectively participate in "political choices that govern one's life [and have] the right of political participation, protection of free speech and association" (Nussbaum 2001, 80). In order to ensure this right, we ought to educate people and give them *real* options in the political realm.

We have the right not to be emotionally or physically violated. Human beings have inherent value. The full worth and dignity granted to each individual dictates that we all ought to be able to live lives free from violence and abuse. Governments ought to protect each citizen's development of capabilities that lead to human flourishing. That would include the fight against an individual's violation of their own rights. Through self-stereotyping, we may come to believe that we do not have certain capabilities, leading us to avoid developing them. If this is the case, then, by my definition, we violate our own rights.

Governments cannot fight against all kinds of cultural practices, social norms, or religious practices. However, if governments provide adequate education and ensure that individuals are able to develop their capabilities to the threshold of functioning, individuals would be less likely to make choices that violate, thwart, or destroy their own capabilities and, hence, their rights.

Beyond Rights

Most people agree that all individuals deserve to enjoy their rights and have the right not to be harmed. However, merely *having* rights is not enough to overcome the harms that oppression has caused in the minds of the oppressed and those who are doing the oppressing. More needs to be done. Research has shown that stereotyping can lead to oppression of a group, but stereotyping also has the potential to help the group out of its oppressive situation. Katherine Reynolds et al. (2000) write that the "stereotyping process can work for social change and resistance to domination just as much as it can contribute to the maintenance of such domination. This is because stereotypes represent context-specific group identities and the current goals and values of group members" (277). In other words, groups can develop an inner-group dynamic that helps them break out of their oppression. This is not simple, and it is a particular challenge for the Iranian American community, which is divided by ethnicity, socioeconomic status, immigration status, level of assimilation, education, and religion. Such divisions are significant enough to prevent a cohesive response to the community's issues. Fragmentation within a group often reduces a group's power, which obstructs or even dismantles progress. We fight against our oppression but, as in any other community, our culture is not monolithic. Coming together with other communities of color that share our various challenges is essential and productive. For instance, Iranian American immigrants struggle with some of the same issues that Mexican American immigrants do. It would be wise to form an alliance addressing immigration challenges.

When we are unable to see a way out of our oppressive situation, we are more motivated to take collective action. Research by Reynolds (2000, 284) and her colleagues concluded that

> In cases in which the group boundary was open [i.e., if people from the oppressed group could enter the world of the powerful], we observed acceptance and stereotype reproduction. However, when the boundaries were firmly closed, participants exhibited a preference for collective protest that represented a strong challenge to the existing status relationship, and this was backed up by creative negative stereotyping of the out-group. . . . [N]egative stereotypes of the powerful group played some determining role in paving the way for social change.

This is extraordinarily important research for diagnosing and understanding oppression in our society and its impact on the psychological state of oppressed minority groups. Two factors are involved in maintaining oppression: (1) whether the oppressed group sees the opportunity for moving from their oppressed situation to the world of the powerful, and (2) which stereotypes the members of the oppressed group collectively hold about the people in power. I will explore these two factors in more detail below.

(1) Can the oppressed change their situation and become *real* members of the social elite class? By "real," I mean not as a token but as a serious agent in the powerful class. As mentioned, some Iranian Americans currently hold positions of political power. According to Reynolds, when the oppressed view the boundaries of the powerful as penetrable, they generally do not collectively rebel against their own oppression. Iranian Americans generally have prospered economically in the United States. We are less likely to support legislation that would provide free legal advice to people who have suffered job discrimination, even though people in our community experience high rates of job discrimination compared to other racial groups. Additionally, the negative stereotypes against our community make us hesitant to become significantly involved in social justice movements. We generally aim to assimilate as much as possible. Additionally, the majority of our community members feel as though their experiences of discrimination are inevitable and isolated, not part of a systematic oppression that the community experiences. And some of us perceive our community challenges to be insignificant compared to the violence that other communities of color experience. Indeed, Iranian American social justice activists often work within other communities

of color, which is beneficial both in creating a more inclusive community and in developing allies.

(2) Stereotyping does not operate in just one direction. People in disadvantaged positions also stereotype those in power, and the specific stereotypes that an oppressed group holds about those in power are associated with the group's willingness to resist its oppression. As long as people believe that those in power do not oppose their advancement in society, they will not collectively act to end their oppression. This is an important point, because Iranian Americans in the United States are not entirely convinced that our oppression is intentional, planned, and systematic. So, for us, the second criterion for collective social change is not met. Consequently, we do not collectively act to end our oppression.

The path to ending racism and racial oppression is bumpy. Martin Luther King, Jr. said that people in power will not give up their power if not challenged. Racial minority leaders often do not challenge the system but instead assimilate to gain access to power. Cudd reminds us that collaborating with our oppressors is not resisting oppression. Yet short-term collaboration might be an essential part of long-term resistance (Cudd 2006, 191–192). She gives us the example of Oskar Schindler who worked for the Nazis to "save Jews from the gas chambers by employing them as slave laborers." Additionally, the reformist works within the system to change the laws to make the situation better, although there is the danger of becoming a part of the system that is oppressive without making any changes in the systems of oppression.

Iranian Americans' privileged socioeconomic status creates an illusion of equality, which is comforting to the privileged groups, but dangerous and damaging to the oppressed. A society in the grip of such illusions ignores its very real racism. Consequently, Iranian Americans minimize the discriminatory conditions under which we live and overlook the social problems that place us in disadvantaged positions. Instead of fixing the system, society ridicules, stereotypes and blames the victims. "[F]ollowing the Reagan and Bush years, American society is back to blaming the victim as an explanation of inequality. . . . The race problem does not lie in the characteristics of Africans [or Iranian Americans], but in the nature of American society" (Van Dyke 1993, 78). Victim-blaming happens when people in privileged groups hold those in disadvantaged groups responsible for their own misfortunes without recognizing the systemic and structural elements that keep them in a subordinate position (Ryan 1976).

GOING FORWARD

The harms of segregation, violence, stereotyping, moral exclusion, injustice, and cultural imperialism have been grave. The situation can be changed, but it will require attention. We can take several measures to minimize racial oppression. The Iranian American community as a whole does not face the challenges of poverty and limited education to the extent that other communities of color might. Although our experiences are significantly different, one situation we have in common with other communities of color is "today's criminalization of people of color, both native-born and immigrants, as well as the criminalization of those who resist oppressive conditions" (Hinson, Healey, Weisenberg, Bester, Sinclair n.d., 7). The historical marginalization and current criminalization of Black and Brown bodies have effects that plague our society. But we can resist by forming intentional alliances with other communities of color, combining our resources, supporting their social justice actions and inviting them to join ours. Our common purpose is to end racial oppression. With more resources, we all have more power to plan, organize, and act.

Relationships among people must be authentic in order to be effective, so we must display integrity in our relationships with other communities of color. We should truly care about the work of social justice as it applies not only to our community, but also to the communities with which we form alliances. Yet regardless of our efforts or our behavior, we will inevitably harm or offend some of our allies on occasion. Therefore, we should start with an honest self-evaluation that includes the courage to address our own biases and the commitment to change them. Rushworth Kidder (2005) reminds us that moral courage is doing the right thing, both internally within our individual selves, and in response to others, even in less-than-ideal circumstances. Change can start only with people who have had an honest self-evaluation and are ready to move forward.

In allied relationships, people will make mistakes, values will come into conflict, and the diversity of people who make up a group will create tension. We must create a clear vision and know our values along with the values of the organization, and be willing to recognize the personalities that we work with. Organizational values should be shared with all members and stakeholders. If an organization's leaders embody its values, it is possible to create a trusting environment. But the Iranian American community, like many other communities of color, is generally not a trusting one. Transparency of goals, purpose, values, and mission are necessary for groups to create trust among people.

Creating change requires us to address all parts of society, because racism has tainted all social structures, including, but not limited to, education, family, housing, mortgage lending, criminal justice, health-care systems, and employment. Education funded by local property taxes might not be sufficient, because it perpetuates inequalities in capabilities development. Likewise, more resources should be allocated to encourage minorities' college attendance. Education is not a panacea, but it remains our most solidly established institutional force for restoration. An educational approach derived from oppressed communities and their experiences is required. Rather than a balanced and calculated response to shelter white sensibilities, we should develop an open pedagogy of the oppressed. In *Pedagogy of the Oppressed,* Paulo Freire (2007, 183) writes,

> The oppressor elaborates his theory of action without the people, for he stands against them. Nor can the people—as long as they are crushed and oppressed, internalizing the image of the oppressor—construct by themselves the theory of their liberating action. Only in the encounter of the people with the revolutionary leader—in their communion, in their praxis—can this theory [a theory of action] be built.

Hence, minority leaders as well as federal support are essential ingredients in ending oppression. The role of government is to create the basis for enhancing the capabilities of individuals and communities, which is also the basis of democratic society.

Inclusion requires that we bring everyone to the table. Our society appears less segregated than in the past, but segregation continues nonetheless. Interpersonal interaction among people of different groups is the most effective way to reduce oppression and discrimination. Direct contact is not necessarily easy; those who feel animosity towards one another will not come to the same table effortlessly. However, invitations to participate in a group's festivities, family celebrations, and community events lead to a familiarity that reduces fear and increases camaraderie. Educational institutions and government organizations can and should pioneer such a movement. Some have already done so, but few such efforts have been undertaken wholeheartedly. Direct contact is not yet a part of the structure of things, but we can take steps to get there. Morton Deutsch (2014, 214) reminds us that we can start by listening to others' experiences.

> Indirect experiences would include conversations with members of an oppressed group about their life experiences; tutored role playing of being a member of such groups; reading autobiographies and novels, watching films and videos which dramatize and make emotionally vivid the experience of injustices; and hearing lectures and sermons which make salient the moral values being violated.

The mass media portrays the Iranian and Iranian American communities as hateful and reprehensible. This is one of the fastest ways that stereotypes are perpetuated. And when the social elite controls the media, as they do in the Unites States, it only makes sense that they preserve the status quo; they have little motivation to change the common portrayal of Iranian Americans. One way to curtail these damaging images would be to create formal, legal ways to challenge the media's negative stereotyping.

We must address the negative society-wide stereotypes against Iranian Americans. But if we are to overcome the effects of self-stereotyping, it is not enough to stop the social stereotypes. We also need serious intervention to get individuals' capabilities to the threshold of functioning so all individuals can enjoy their rights. Racial socialization starts at a very young age. We are taught our roles, which to some extent define the way we self-identify and realize our abilities or lack thereof. Therefore, if we are to counter the negative stereotypes in our society, we should start with children when they are very young. To do this effectively in impoverished areas, we must take seriously the education of racial minority children. Many schools need better funding as well as programs to create inclusivity, tolerance, and moral sensitivity.

Our fight to end oppression should target not only future citizens but also the children and adults who are negatively affected by racism and stereotype threats right now. I suggest that, despite the difficulty of the task, we as a society ought to aim at reversing the stereotypes and reconstructing capabilities that have been damaged. The restoration of undermined capabilities is our critical project here. Influential social figures and community leaders play key roles and are essential in starting the movement in peaceful but radical ways. Groups that aim to empower the oppressed should gain public support, rather than being dismissed and labeled *domestic terrorists,* a phenomenon that Iranian Americans encounter all too frequently. For instance, Iranian American cultural groups often find themselves questioned by government officials to determine whether they are somehow morally corrupt or pawns of the Islamic Republic.

In a democratic society, it is shameful to allow racial divisions to persist and to permit so many voices to go unheard. People of color should have input in lawmaking and policy-making. Our society can make this happen by removing barriers to political participation and by increasing access to engagement in policy development. The Iranian American community in Oklahoma routinely invites local politicians to participate in our cultural events, not only to create community but also to humanize ourselves. We have been so dehumanized by our portrayal in the mass media over the last forty years that we must first erase society's negative images of us before our political demands will be heard. In essence, we must create trust and expand the moral scope of those around us to include the Iranian American community. That is best done by building communities and establishing relationships.

Simultaneously, we ought to rebuild people's capabilities that have been destroyed and aim to get everyone to the threshold level of functioning, both mentally and physically. This is not an impossible task. In his book *Learned Optimism*, Martin Seligman (1990) explains the psychology behind optimistic and pessimistic attitudes and expectations. Pessimistic attitudes and expectations can prevent people from resisting and overcoming oppressive situations. An optimistic perception of self, on the other hand, helps create possibilities. It is important for me to emphasize that I am not reducing the oppression of racial minorities to an "attitude problem," but instead pointing out that to stop racial oppression, we must undermine the patterns of thought and feeling that produce voluntary oppression. Reducing oppressive patterns of thoughts is an obvious first step; only then will we have a reasonable chance of making progress toward ending the oppression of racial minorities.

Bibliography

Abdi, Jamal. "Iranian Americans Increasingly at the Center of Systemic Discrimination Across the U.S." *National Iranian American Council* (November 15, 2019). Niacouncil.org. www.niacouncil.org/iranian-americans-increasingly-center-systematic-discrimination-across-u-s/ (accessed December 14, 2019).

Alcoff, Linda Martin. "Philosophy and Racial Identity." in *Radical Philosophy* 75 (January/February 1996): 5–14.

Ander, Judith. "Power, Oppression and Gender." *Social Theory and Practice: An International and Interdisciplinary Journal of Social Philosophy* 11, no. 1 (Spring 1985): 107–122.

Anzaldua, Gloria. *Borderlands/La Frontera: The New Mestiza,* 4th ed. San Francisco: Aunt Lute Books, 2007.

Appiah, Kwame Anthony. "'But Would That Still Be Me?'" Notes on Gender, 'Race,' Ethnicity, as Sources of 'Identity'." *The Journal of Philosophy* 87, no. 10, Eighty-Seventh Annual Meeting American Philosophical Association, Eastern Division, October, 1990.

———. *Race, Culture, Identity: Misunderstood Connections*. The Tanner Lectures on Human Values, Delivered at the University of California in San Diego (October 27–28, 1994): 1–86.

———. "Racism." in *Anatomy of Racism.* Edited by David Theo Goldberg, Minneapolis: University of Minnesota Press, 1990: 3–17.

———. Stanford Presidential Lectures in the Humanities and Arts (2004). prelectur.stanford.edu/lecturers/appiah/index.html (accessed January 2, 2020).

———. "The Uncompleted Argument: Du Bois and the Illusion of Race." in *Critical Inquiry* 12, no. 1 (Autumn 1985): 21–37.

Aristotle, *Nicomachean Ethics,* chapter III, 1111a10. Translated by Terence Irwin. Indiana: Hackett Publishing Company, 1985.

Arneson, Richard. "Perfectionism and Politics." *Ethics* 111, no. 1 (October 2000): 37–63.

Bailey, Alison. "Privilege: Expanding on Merilyn Frye's 'Oppression'." *Journal of Social Philosophy* 29, no. 3 (Winter 98): 104–119.

Bandura, Albert. *Social Learning Theory*. New York: General Learning Press: 1977.

Bartky, Sandra L. *Femininity and Domination: Studies in the Phenomenology of Oppression*. New York: Routledge Publishing, 1990.

Basu, Moni. "15 Years After 9/11, Sikhs Still Victims of Anti-Muslim Hate Crime." in CNN.com (September, 15, 2016). www.cnn.com/2016/09/15/us/sikh-hate-crime-victims/index.html (accessed October 2019).

Beeghly, Erin. "What is a Stereotype? What is Stereotyping?" *Hypatia*, 30, no. 4 (Fall 2015): 675–691.

Bernstein, Mark H. *On Moral Considerability*. New York: Oxford University Press, 1998.

Blum, Lawrence. "Stereotypes and Stereotyping: A Moral Analysis." *Philosophical Papers* 33, no. 3 (2004): 251–289.

Bonilla-Silva, Eduardo. *Racism Without Racists: Colorblind Racism and the Persistence of Racial Inequality in America* 4th ed. New York: Rowman & Littlefield Publishers, Inc., 2013.

Brison, Susan J. *Aftermath: Violence and Remaking of a Self.* Princeton University Press, 2003.

Brown, Stuart L. "The Consequence of Play Deprivation." *Scholarpedia* 9, no. 5. www.scholarpedia.org/article/Consequences_of_Play_Deprivation (accessed October 2019).

Burchardt, Tania, and Rod Hick. "Inequality, Advantage and the Capability Approach." *Journal of Human Development and Capabilities* 19, no. 1 (2018): 38–52.

Bush, George W. "Text of President Bush's 2002 State of the Union Address." *The Washington Post* (January 29, 2002). www.washingtonpost.com/wp-srv/onpolitics/transcripts/sou012902.htm (accessed on November 5, 2019).

Canby, Vicent. "Review/Film; Sally Field, Fervently: Not Without My Daughter." *New York Times* (January, 11, 1991). www.nytimes.com/1991/01/11/movies/review-film-sally-field-fervently.html (accessed on November 5, 2019).

Carter, James E. "President Carter's Speech." *Iran Hostage Crisis* (January 23, 1980). iranhostagecrisishdp1.weebly.com/president-carters-speech.html (accessed November 4, 2019).

Census Glossary. U.S. Department of Commerce: Economic and Statistics Administration. www.census.gov/glossary/#term_White (accessed December 11, 2019).

Charlesworth, Hilary. "Martha Nussbaum's Feminist Internationalism." *Ethics* 111, no. 1 (October 2000): 64–78.

Chegeni, Maryam, Atiyeh Kamel Khodabandeh, Mohammad Karamouzian, Mostafa Shokoohi, Leili Abedi, Malahat Khalili, Leila Rajaei, Gelayol Ardalan, and Hamid Sharifi. "Alcohol Consumption in Iran: A Systematic Review and Meta-Analysis of the Literature." *Drug and Alcohol Review* 39, no. 5 (July 2020): 525–538. (first published online in May 22, 2020 onlinelibrary.wiley.com/doi/abs/10.1111/dar.13093)

Cheng, Amrit. *Fact-Checking Family Separation.* www.aclu.org/blog/immigrants-qrights/immigrants-rights-and-detention/fact-checking-family-separation (Accessed October 22, 2019).

Chubin, Fae. "When My Virtue Defends Your Borders: Political Justification of Nation and Order Through the Rhetorical Production of Womanhood in the 1979 Islamic Revolution of Iran." *Women Studies International Forum* 42 (2014): 44–55.

Collins, Patricia Hill. *Black feminist thought: Knowledge, Consciousness, and the Politics of Empowerment,* 2nd ed. New York: Routledge, 2000.

Cook, Joyce Mitchell. Paper delivered at Philosophy and the Black Liberation Struggle Conference, University of Illinois, Chicago Circle, November 19–20, 1970, as quoted in Bartky, Sandra. "On Psychological Oppression."*Femininity and Domination: Studies in the Phenomenology of Oppression.* New York: Routledge, 1990.

Cottingham, John. "Integrity and Fragmentation." *Journal of Applied Philosophy* 27, no. 1. 2010: 2–14.

Cox, Damian, Marguerite La Caze and Michael Levine. "Integrity." *The Sandford Encyclopedia of Philosophy.* Edited by Edward N. Zalta. Standford University: Spring 2017.

Cross, William E. Jr. *Shades of Black: Diversity in African-American Identity.* Philadelphia: Temple University Press, 1991.

Cudd, Ann E. *Analyzing Oppression.* New York: Oxford University Press, 2006.

———. "Missionary Positions." in *Hypatia* 20, no. 4 (Fall 2005): 164–182.

———. "Oppression by Choice." *Journal of Social Philosophy* 25, no. 1 (June 1994): 22–44.

———. "Psychological Explanations of Oppression." *Theorizing Multiculturalism: A Guide to the Current Debate.* Edited by Cynthia Willett. Massachusetts: Blackwell Publishing, 1998: 187–216.

Darby, Derrick. "Blacks and Rights: A Bittersweet Legacy." *Law, Culture, and the Humanities* 2 (2006): 436–437.

Dawsey, Josh. "Trump Derides Protection for Immigrants from 'Shithole' Countries." *Washington Post* (January 12, 2018) www.washingtonpost.com/politics/trump-attacks-protections-for-immigrants-from-shithole-countries-in-oval-office-meeting/2018/01/11/bfc0725c-f711-11e7-91af-31ac729add94_story.html (accessed November 20, 2019).

DeGruy, Joy. *Post Traumatic Slave Syndrome* (Revised edition). Uptone Press and Joy DeGruy Publications, 2017.

Deutsch, Morton. "Justice and Conflict." *Conflict, Interdependence, and Justice.* Edited by Peter T. Coleman. New York, Springer: 2011. 193–226.

———. "A Framework for Thinking about Oppression and Its Change." *Conflict, Interdependence, and Justice.* Edited by Peter T. Coleman. New York, Springer: 2011. 95–118.

Domonokse, Camila, and Richard Gonzales. "What We Know: Family Separations and 'Zero Tolerance' At the Border." (June 19, 2018). www.npr.org/2018/06/19/621065383/what-we-know-family-separation-and-zero-tolerance-at-the-border (accessed October 22, 2019).

Donnelly, Jack. "Human Rights as Natural Rights." *Human Rights Quarterly* 4, no. 3 (Autumn 1982): 395–397.

Dumas, Firoozeh. *Funny in Farsi: A Memoir of Growing up Iranian in America.* New York: Random House, 2004.

Dworkin, Ronald. *Taking Rights Seriously.* Cambridge: Harvard University Press, 1978.

Elahi, Babak, and Persis M. Karim. "Introduction: Iranian Diaspora." *Comparative Studies of South Asia, Africa and the Middle East* 31, no. 2 (2011): 381–387.

Emami, Jessica (2014), *Iranian Americans: Immigration and Assimilation* (report). Washington, DC: Public Affairs Alliance of Iranian Americans, 2014.

Emery, Sean. "White Supremacist Gang Member Convicted of Fatal Stabbing at Laguna Niguel Bar." *Orange County Register* (December 18, 2019). Ocregister.com. www.ocregister.com/2019/12/18/white-supremacist-gang-member-convicted-of-fatal-stabbing-at-laguna-niguel-bar/ (accessed December 29, 2019).

Espiritu, Yen Le. "A Critical Transnational Perspective to Asian America." *The Oxford Handbook of Philosophy and Race.* Edited by Naomi Zack. New York: Oxford University Press, 2017: 102–113.

Exec. Order no. 13,780, F.R. 04837 (2017). Protecting the Nation from Foreign Terrorist Entry Into the United States. www.federalregister.gov/documents/2017/03/09/2017-04837/protecting-the-nation-from-foreign-terrorist-entry-into-the-united-states

Feinberg, Joel. *Social Philosophy.* New Jersey: Prentice-Hall, 1973.

———. "The Nature and Value of Rights." *Journal of Value Inquiry* 4, no. 4 (Winter 1970): 243–260.

Freire, Paulo. *Pedagogy of the Oppressed,* 30th Anniversary Edition. Translated by Myra Bergman Ramos. New York: Continuum, 2007.

Fricker, Miranda. *Epistemic Injustice: Power & the Ethics of Knowing.* London: Oxford University Press, 2007.

Frye, Marilyn. "Oppression." *Politics of Reality: Essays in Feminist Theory.* New York: The Crossing Press, 1983: 1–16.

Gaylord-Harden, Noni K., Suzanna So, Grace J. Bai, and Patrick H. Tolan. "Examining the Effects of Emotional and Cognitive Desensitization to Community Violence Exposure in Male Adolescents of Color." *American Journal of Orthopsychiatry* 87, no. 4 (2017): 463–473.

Gewirth, Alan. "Are All Rights Positive Rights?" *Philosophy and Public Affairs* 30, no. 3 (Summer 2001): 321–333.

Ghandehari, Alborz. "Iranian Americans Victims of Unjust Discrimination." *The Salt Lake Tribune* (September 12, 2019). www.sltrib.com/opinion/commentary/2019/11/12/alborz-ghandehari-iranian/ (accessed December 1, 2019).

Ghavami, Negin, and Letitia Ann Peplau. "An Intersectional Analysis of Gender and Ethnic Stereotypes: Testing Three Hypotheses." *Psychology of Women Quarterly,* 37 (2012): 113–127.

Goodpaster, Kenneth. "On Being Morally Considerable." *Journal of Philosophy* 75 (1978): 308–325.

Gould, Stephen Jay. *The Mismeasure of Man.* New York: W. W. Norton and Company, 1981.
Gracia, Jorge J. E. "Race and Ethnicity." *The Oxford Handbook of Philosophy and Race.* Edited by Naomi Zack. New York: Oxford University Press, 2017: 180–194.
———. *Surviving Race, Ethnicity, and Nationality: A Challenge for the 21st Century.* Lanham, MD: Rowman & Littlefield Publishers, Inc., 2005.
Hadid, Diaa and Khwaga Ghani. "Women and Children Are The Emerging Face Of Drug Addiction In Afghanistan." *National Public Radio.* (October 29, 2019): www.npr.org/sections/goatsandsoda/2019/10/29/771374889/women-and-children-are-the-emerging-face-of-drug-addiction-in-afghanistan
Hahn, Hyeouk Chris, Judith G. Gonyea, Christine Chiao, and Luca Anna Koritsanszky. "Fractured Identity: Framework for Understanding Young Asian American Women's Self-Harm and Suicidal Behaviors." *Race and Social Problems* 6, no. 1 (2014, January 22 online version; March 2014): 56–68.
Harding, Sandra. *Whose Science? Whose Knowledge?: Thinking from Women's Lives.* New York: Cornell University Press, 1991.
———. "Socially Relevant Philosophy of Science? Resources from Standpoint Theory's Controversiality." in *Hypatia* 19, no. 1 (Winter 2004): 25–47.
———. *The Feminist Standpoint Reader* (ed.), New York: Routledge, 2004a.
Harvey, Jean. *Civilized Oppression.* Oxford: Rowman & Littlefield Publishers, Inc., 1999.
Haslanger, Sally. "Gender and Race: (What) Are they? (What) Do We Want Them To Be?" *Nous* 34, no. 1 (2000): 31–55.
———. "Language, Politics, and 'The Folk': Looking for 'The Meaning' of 'Race'." *The Monist* 93, no. 2 (April 2010): 169–187.
———. "You Mixed?" *Adoption Matters: Philosophical and Feminist Essays.* Edited by Sally Haslanger, and Charlotte Witt. Ithaca: Cornell University Press, 2005.
Hassanian-Moghaddam, Hossein and Nasim Zamani. "Suicide in Iran: The Facts and Figures from Nationwide Report." *Iranian Journal of Psychiatry* 12, no. 1 (January 2017): 73–77. www.ncbi.nlm.nih.gov/pmc/articles/PMC5425355/ (accessesd August 21, 2020).
Health Inequalities Manifesto, prepared by Mental Health Foundation. London, England: 2018. www.mentalhealth.org.uk/publications/health-inequalities-manifesto-2018 (accessed January 27, 2020).
Hegel, Georg W. F. *Philosophy of Mind,* trans. W. Wallace. Oxford: Clarendon Press, 1971.
Helliwell, John F. "Global Happiness Policy Synthesis." *Global Happiness Policy Report,* 2018: 10–25. www.worldgovernmentsummit.org/api/publications/document?id=304a8bc4-e97c-6578-b2f8-ff0000a7ddb6 (accessed January 27, 2020).
Hembree, Diana. "Bank of America Accused of Discriminating Against Iranian Americans." *Forbes Magazine* (May 22, 2018). www.forbes.com/sites/dianahembree/2018/05/22/bank-of-america-accused-of-discrimination-against-iranian-americans/#752592871d92 (accessed on November 2, 2019).

Hinson, Sandra, Richard Healey, Nathaniel Weisenberg, DeAngelo Bester, and Charlene Sinclair. *Race, Power, and Policy: Dismantling Structural Racism.* Prepared for National People's Action by the Grassroots Policy Project with cooperation with National People's Action and Union Theological Seminary. (n.d.): 1–38. www.racialequitytools.org/resourcefiles/race_power_policy_workbook.pdf (accessed December 15, 2019).

Hobbes, Thomas. *Leviathan.* Edited by C. B. Macpherson. New York: Penguin Books, 1985. Originally published in 1707.

hooks, bell. "Homeplace: A Site of Resistance." *Yearning: Race, Gender, and Cultural Politics.* London: Turnaround Publishing, 1991.

Howard, Judith A. "The 'Normal' Victim: The Effects of Gender Stereotypes on Reactions to Victims." *Social Psychology Quarterly* 47, no. 3 (September 1984): 270–281.

Ibrahim, Solva, and Meera Tiwari (eds). *The Capability Approach: From Theory to Practice.* Basingstoke: Palgrave MacMillan, 2014.

Internet Movie Database. *Shahs of Sunset.* www.imdb.com/title/tt1997999/ (accessed June 20, 2016).

Jackman, Tom. "Fairfax Prosecutors Seeking Indictments Against Park Police Officers in Fatal Shooting of Bijan Ghaisar." *Washington Post* (December 19, 2019). Washingtonpost.com. www.washingtonpost.com/crime-law/2019/12/18 fairfax-prosecutors-seeking-indictments-against-park-police-officers-fatal-shooting-bijan-ghaisar/ (accessed December 20, 2019).

Jacobs, David, and Robert M. O'Brien. "The Determinants of Deadly Force: A Structural Analysis of Police Violence." *The American Journal of Sociology* 103, no. 4. (January 1998): 837–862.

Jost, John T, and Mahzarin R. Banaji. "The Role of Stereotyping in System-Justification and the Production of False Consciousness." *British Journal of Social Psychology* 33, no. 1, (March 1994): 1–27.

Kane, Thomas J. *Race, College Attendance, and College Completion.* Washington DC: Brookings Institution, (September 1994): 1–38. /eric.ed.gov/?id=ED374766 (accessed January 2, 2020).

Khader, Serene. *Adaptive Preferences and Women's Empowerment.* New York: Oxford University Press, 2011.

Kidder, Rushworth M. *Moral Courage.* New York: Harper Collins Publishers, 2005.

King, Martin Luther, Jr. "Letter from Birmingham Jail." *Atlantic Monthly: The Negro Is Your Brother* 212, no. 2 (August 1963): 78–88. web.cn.edu/kwheeler/documents/Letter_Birmingham_Jail.pdf

King, Ryab D. and Darren Wheelock. "Group Threat and Social Control: Race, Perception of Minorities and the Desire to Punish" *Social Forces* 85, no. 3 (March 2007): 1255–1280.

Krever, Mick. "Brain Drain to the West: Why Iran's Brightest Young Graduates Are Leaving Their Country Behind." CNN.com (June 27, 2017). www.cnn.com/2017/06/27/middleeast/irans-mit-sharif-university-technology/index.html (accessed December 30, 2019).

LaBossiere, Michael C. "Racial Identity and Oppression." *International Journal of Applied Philosophy* 11, no. 2 (Winter 1997): 31–38.

Lanard, Noah. "Ice is Sending Asylum-Seekers to the Private Prisons Where Mother Jones Exposed Abuse." *Mother Jones* (June 11, 2019). www.motherjones.com/politics/2019/06/ice-is-sending-asylum-seekers-to-the-private-prison-where-mother-jones-exposed-abuse/ (accessed 1/6/2020).

Lane, Anthony. "Film Within a Film: 'Argo' and 'Sinister'." *New Yorker* (October 8, 2012). www.newyorker.com/arts/critics/cinema/2012/10/15/121015crci_cinema_lane (accessed November 5, 2019).

Levy-Pounds, Nekima. "Vulnerable Population: Par for the Course?: Exploring the Impacts of Incarceration and Marginalization on Poor Black Men in the U.S." *Journal of Law in Society* 14, no 1 (Winter 2013): 29–309.

Locke, John. Second Treaties of Government. Edited by C. B. Macpherson. Indianapolis: Hackett Publishing Company, 1980. Originally published in 1690.

Loots, Sonja, and Melanie Walker. "A Capabilities-Based Gender Equality Policy for Higher Education: Conceptual and Methodological Considerations." *Journal of Human Development and Capabilities* 17, no. 2 (2016): 260–277.

Lopez, Ian F. Haney. *White by Law: The Legal Construction of Race.* New York University Press: 1996.

Lugones, Maria. "Playfulness, 'World'-Travelling, and Loving Perception." *Hypatia* 2, no. 2 (Summer, 1987): 3–19.

Maghbouleh, Neda. *The Limits of Whiteness: Iranian Americans and the Everyday Politics of Race.* California: Stanford University Press, 2017.

Mahdavi, Sara. "Held Hostage: Identity Citizenship of Iranian Americans." *Texas Journal on Civil Liberties and Civil Rights* 11, no 2 (Spring 2006): 211–244.

Mallon, Ron. "Racial Identity Racial Ontology, and Racial Norms." *The Oxford Handbook of Philosophy and Race.* Edited by Naomi Zack. New York: Oxford University Press, 2017: 392–409.

———. "Traveling and Reality: Social Constructionism and the Metaphysics of Race." *Nous* 38, no. 4 (December 2004): 644–673.

Mappes, Thomas A. "Sexual Morality and the Concept of Using Another Person." *Social Ethics: Morality and Social Policy,* 4th edition. Edited by Thomas A. Mappes and Jane S. Zembaty. New York: McGraw-Hill Inc., 1992: 207–223.

Martin, Rex. *A System of Rights.* Oxford: Clarendon Press, 1993.

Martinez, Karen, G. and Jessica Graham-LoPresti. "The Effects of Racism on Mental Health: How to Cope" (Webinar). *Anxiety and Depression Association of America*: August, 7, 2018: adaa.org/webinar/consumer/effects-racism-mental-health-how-cope (accessed January 27, 2020.

McKinnon, Rachel. "Allies Behaving Badly: Gaslighting as Epistemic Injustice." *The Routledge Handbook of Epistemic Injustice.* Edited by Ian James Kidd, Jose Medina, and Gaile Pohlhause Jr. New York: Taylor and Francis Group, 2017.

Michaels, Walter Benn. *Race into Culture: A Critical Genealogy of Cultural Identity. Cultural Inquiry* 18. (1992): 655–685.

———. "The No-Drop Rule." in *Critical Inquiry* 20 (1994): 758–769

Mills, Charles. *Blackness Visible: Essays on Philosophy and Race*. Ithaca: Cornell University Press, 1998.

Mitchell, Stephanie, and Cynthia Ronzio. "Violence and Other Stressful Life Events as Triggers of Depression and Anxiety: What Psychosocial Resources Protect African American Mothers?" *Maternal and Child Health Journal* 15, no. 8 (2011): 1272–1281.

Moaveni, Azadeh. *Lipstick Jihad: A Memoir of Growing up Iranian in American and American in Iran*. Public Affairs: 2007.

Mobasher, Mohsen. *The Iranian Diaspora: Challenges, Negotiations, and Transformations*. Texas: University of Texas Press, 2018.

———. *Iranians in Texas: Migration, Politics, and Ethnic Identity*. Austin: University of Texas Press, 2012.

Montague, Phillip. "Two Concepts of Rights." *Philosophy and Public Affairs* 9, no. 3 (Summer 1980): 372–384.

Moses, Michele. "The Relationship Between Self-Determination, the Social Context of Choice, and Authenticity." *Philosophy of Education,* 2000.

Mostashari, Ali, and Ali Khodamhosseini. *An Overview of Socioeconomic Characteristics of the Iranian-American Community based on the 2000 U.S. Census* (February 2004). bahmani.com/iasurvey/other_surveys/MIT_demographics.pdf (accessed January 5, 2020).

Nagel, Thomas. *The View from Nowhere*. Oxford: Oxford University Press,1986.

Nelson, Julia A. "Freedom, Reason, and More: Feminist Economics and Human Development." *Journal of Human Development* 5, no. 3 (November 2004): 309–333.

Nozick, Robert. *Anarchy, State, and Utopia*. New York: Basic Books,1974.

Nuccetelli, Susana. "Reference and Ethnic-Group Terms." In *Inquiry: An Interdisciplinary Journal of Philosophy* 47, no. 6 (December 2004): 528–544.

Nussbaum, Martha. "Aristotle, Politics, and Human Capabilities." *Ethics* 111 (October 2000a): 102–140.

———. *Sex and Social Justice*. London: Oxford University Press, 2000.

———. *Women and Human Development*. Cambridge: Cambridge University Press, 2001.

Opotow, Susan, Janet Gerson, and Sarah Woodside. "From Moral Exclusion to Moral Inclusion: Theory for Teaching Peace." *Theory Into Practice* 44, no. 4 (Autumn 2005): 301–318.

Ortega, Mariana. *In-Between: Latina Feminist Phenomenology, Multiplicity, and the Self*. New York: State University of New York, 2016.

Outlaw, Lucius. "On W.E.B. Du Bois's 'The Conservation of Races'." *Overcoming Racism and Sexism*. Edited by Linda A. Bell, and David Blumenfeld. New York, Rowman & Littlefield Publishers, Inc., 1995: 79–102.

———. *On Race and Philosophy*. New York: Routledge, 1996.

———. "Toward a Critical Theory of 'Race'." *The Anatomy of Racism*. Edited by David Theo Goldberg. Minneapolis: University of Minnesota Press, 1990: 58–82.

Paige, Shari, Elaine Hatfield, and Lu Liang. "Iranian-American's Perceptions of Prejudice and Discrimination: Differences Between Muslim, Jewish, and Non-

Religious Iranian-Americans." *Interpersona: An International Journal on Personal Relations* 9, no. 2 (2015): 236–252.
Pateman, Carol. "Feminism and Democracy." *Democratic Theory and Practice.* Cambridge: Cambridge University Press, 1985: 204–217.
Peffer, Rodney. "A Defense of Rights to Well-Being." *Philosophy and Public Affairs* 8, no. 1 (Autumn 1978): 65–87.
Pereira, Roseanne. "Valarie Kaur's Search for America after 9/11." NPR.org (April 3, 2007). minnesota.publicradio.org/display/web/2007/04/03/sikhfilm/ (accessed September 20, 2019).
Phillips, Anne. "Feminism and Liberalism Revisited: Has Martha Nussbaum Got It Right?" *Constellations* 8, no. 2 (June 2001): 249–266.
Piper, Adrian. "Passing for White, Passing for Black." *Transition* 58, (1992): 4–32.
Puddifoot, Katherine. "Stereotyping: The Multifactorial View." *Philosophical Topics* 45, no. 1, (Spring 2017): 137–156.
Ramos, Andrew. "NYC Marathon Runner Ridiculed, Called 'Dirty Muslim' as He Ran Race." *Pix 11.* (November 7, 2016). pix11.com/2016/11/07/nyc-marathon-runner-ridiculed-called-dirty-muslim-as-he-ran-26-mile-race/
Rawls, John. *Justice as Fairness: A Restatement.* Edited by Erin Kelly. Cambridge: The Belknap Press of Harvard University Press, 2003.
———. *Political Liberalism.* New York: Columbia University Press, 1993.
———. *The Law of Peoples.* Massachusetts: Harvard University Press, 2000.
Reilly, Katie. "Here Are All the Times Donald Trump Insulted Mexico." *Time* (August 31, 2016). time.com/4473972/donald-trumpmexico-meeting-insult/ (accessed on August 3, 2019).
Reynolds, Katherine J., Penelope J. Oakes, S. Alexander Haslam, Mark A. Nolan, and Larissa Dolnik, "Responses to Powerlessness: Stereotyping as an Instrument of Social Conflict." *Group Dynamics: Theory, Research, and Practice* 4 (2000): 275–290.
Rivera, Lisa. "Aspirations and Morality: Williams Reconsidered." *Ethical Theory and Moral Practice* 10, no. 1 (February 2007): 69–87.
Root, Michael. "How We Divide the World." *Philosophy of Social Science Proceedings* 67 (2000): 628–639
Rousseau, Jean-Jacques. *Social Contract.* Translated by Donald A. Cress. Indianapolis, Hackett Publishing Company: 1987.
Ryan, William. *Blaming the Victim.* New York: Vintage Publishers, 1976.
Sanger, David E. "Iran Complies with Nuclear Deal; Sanctions Are Lifted." *New York Times.* (January 16, 2016). www.nytimes.com/2016/01/17/world/middleeast/iran-sanctions-lifted-nuclear-deal.html (accessed September 5, 2019).
Sediqi, Sataruddin. "The Impact of Addiction on Afghan Youth." *Intervention: Journal of Mental Health and Psychosocial Support in Conflict Affected Areas* 16, no. 3 (2018): 283–286.
Seligman, Martin. *Learned Optimism.* New York: Vintage Books, 1990.
Sen, Amartya. "Freedoms and Needs." *The New Republic* (January 10, 2017, 1994): 31–38.
———. *Development as Freedom.* New York: Anchor Books, 2000.

———. Inequality Reexamined. Cambridge, MA: Harvard University Press, 1992.

———. "Rights and Agency." *Philosophy and Public Affairs* 11, no. 1 (1982): 3–39.

———. "Rights and Capabilities." *Resources, Values and Development*. Cambridge: Harvard University Press, 1984: 307–324.

——— "The Standard of Living." *The Standard of Living: The Tanner Lectures on Human Values*, Cambridge: Cambridge University Press, 1987.

Shelby, Tommie. "Foundations of Black Solidarity: Collective Identity or Common Oppression." *Ethics* 112, no. 2 (January 2002): 231–266.

Sheth, Falguni A. "The Radicalization of Muslims in the Post-9/11 United States." *The Oxford Handbook of Philosophy and Race*. Edited by Naomi Zack. New York: Oxford University Press, 2017: 342–351.

Shue, Henry. *Basic Rights*. Princeton: Princeton University Press, 1980.

Smith, Andrew. "Food Deserts, Capabilities, and the Rectification of Democratic Failure." *Journal of Human Development and Capabilities* 17, no. 2 (2016): 178–190.

Smith, Tara. "On Deriving Rights to Goods from Rights to Freedom." *Law and Philosophy* 11, no. 3 (Winter 1992): 217–234.

Soparvaz, Tehran. *Persian is the New Black* (Video). (August 16, 2013). www.youtube.com/watch?v=lxO5pWNVWY4 (accessed on November 5, 2019).

St. Aimee, Joshua. "When It Comes to St. Lucian Citizenship, Iran Need Not Apply." *The Star*, (August 19, 2018). https://stluciastar.com/when-it-comes-to-st-lucian-citizenship-iran-need-not-apply/ (accessed on December 1, 2019).

Stark, Susan. "Taking Responsibility for Oppression: Affirmative Action and Racial Injustice." *Public Affairs Quarterly* 18, no. 3, (July 2004): 205–221.

Steele, Claude. "Thin Ice: Stereotype Threat and Black College Students." *The Atlantic* (August 1999). www.theatlantic.com/magazine/archive/1999/08/thin-ice-stereotype-threat-and-black-college-students/304663/ (accessed on September 14, 2019).

———, and Joshua Aronson. "Stereotype Threat and the Intellectual Test Performance of African Americans." *Journal of Personality and Social Psychology* 69, no. 5 (November 1995): 797–811.

Stringer, Heather. "Psychologists Respond to a Mental Health Crisis at the Border" *The Monitor* 49, no. 8 (September 2018). www.apa.org/monitor/2018/09/crisis-border (accessed October 23, 2019).

Tatum, Beverly. *"Why are all the Black Kids Sitting Together in the Cafeteria?" and Other Conversations About Race*. New York: Basic Books, 1997.

Taylor, Paul. *Race: A Philosophical Introduction*. Massachusetts: Polity Press, 2013.

Tehranian, John. *Whitewashed: America's Invisible Middle-Eastern Minority*. New York: New York University Press, 2009.

Terzi, Lorella. "Beyond the Dilemma of Difference: The Capability Approach to Disability and Special Needs." *Journal of Philosophy of Education* 39, no. 3 (2005): 443–459.

———. "Capabilities and Education Equality: The Just Distribution of Resources to Students with Disabilities and Special Education Needs." *Journal of Philosophy of Education* 41, no. 4 (2007): 757–773.

Torbat, Akbar. "The Brain Drain from Iran to the United States." *Middle East Journal,* 56, no. 2 (Spring 2002): 272–295.
Trent, Maria, Danielle G. Dooley, and Jacqueline Douge. "The Impact of Racism on Child and Adolescent Health." *Pediatrics* 144, no. 2 (August 2019): 1–14.
Vallentyne, Peter. "Debate: Capabilities Versus Opportunities for Well-Being." *Journal of Political Philosophy* 13, no. 3 (2005): 359–371.
Van Dyke, Sandra "The Evaluation of Race Theory: A Perspective" *Journal of Black Studies* 24, no. 1 (September, 1993): 77–87.
Vasquez, Jessica. "Blurred Borders for Some but Not 'Others': Racialization, 'Flexible Ethnicity,' Gender, and Third-Generation Mexican American Identity." *Sociological Perspectives* 53, no. 1 (Spring 2010): 45–72.
Venkatapuram, Sridhar. "Mental Disability, Human Rights, and the Capabilities Approach: Searching for the Foundations." *International Review of Psychiatry* 26, no. 4 (August 2014): 408–414.
Vernado, Victor. "What Growing Up as a Black Albino Taught Me." In *Vice* (February 15, 2018). www.vice.com/en_us/article/pamkan/what-growing-up-as-a-black-albino-taught-me (accessed September 10, 2019).
Walters, Karina L., Selina A. Mohammed, Teresa Evans-Campbell, Ramona E. Beltran, David H. Chae, and Bonnie Duran. "Bodies Don't Just Tell Stories, They Tell Histories: Embodiment of Historical Trauma Among American Indians and Alaska Natives." *Du Bois Review: Social Science Research on Race* 8, no. 1 (2011): 179–189.
White, Ralph K. *Nobody Wanted War*. Garden City: Anchor Books, 1970.
Williams, Bernard. "The Standard of Living; Interests and Capabilities." in *The Standard of Living,* edited by G. Hawthorne. Cambridge: Cambridge University Press, 1987.
Williams, Patricia. *The Alchemy of Race and Rights.* Cambridge: Harvard University Press, 1991.
Wylie, Alison. "Why Standpoint Matters." *Science and Other Cultures: Issues in Philosophies of Sciences and Technology.* Edited by Albert Figueroa and Sandra Harding. New York: Routledge, 2003.
Yancy, George. *Black Bodies, White Gaze: The Continuing Significance of Race.* Colorado: Rowman & Littlefield Publishers, Inc., 2008.
———. "The Violent Weight of Whiteness: The Existential and Psychic Price Paid by Black Male Bodies." *The Oxford Handbook of Philosophy and Race.* Edited by Naomi Zack. New York: Oxford University Press, 2017: 587–597.
———. and Zack, Naomi. "What 'White Privilege' Really Means." *New York Times*. (November 5, 2014). opinionator.blogs.nytimes.com/2014/11/05/what-white-privilege-really-means/#more-154773 (accessed September 10, 2019).
Young, Iris. "Five Faces of Oppression." *The Philosophical Forum* 19, no. 4 (1988): 270–290.
———. *Justice and the Politics of Difference*. Princeton: Princeton University Press, 1990.

Zack, Naomi. "Ideal, Nonideal, and Empirical Theories of Social Justice." *The Oxford Handbook of Philosophy and Race.* Edited by Naomi Zack. New York: Oxford University Press, 2017: 548–559.

———. *Philosophy of Science and Race.* New York: Routledge, 2002.

———. "The Fluid Symbol of Mixed Race." *Hypatia* 25, no. 4 (Fall 2010). 875–890.

———. *Race and Mixed Race.* Philadelphia: Temple University, 1993.

———. *White Privilege and black Rights: The Injustice of U.S. Police Racial Profiling and Homicide.* Lanham, MD: Rowman & Littlefield Publishers, Inc., 2015.

Zarroli, Jim. "Study: Upward Mobility No Tougher in U.S. Than Two Decades Ago." *National Public Radio.* (January 23, 2014). www.npr.org/2014/01/23/265356290/study-upward-mobility-no-tougher-in-u-s-than-two-decades-ago (accessed August 20, 2020).

Zutlevics, T. L. "Relational Selves, Personal Autonomy and Oppression." *Philosophia* 29, no. 1–4 (January 2002a): 423–436.

———. "Towards a Theory of Oppression." *Ratio* 15, no. 1 (March 2002b): 80–102.

Index

African Americans: albino, racial identity challenges for, 34; cultural identity for, 46–47; ethnicity and, 39–40; identity based on shared culture, 24; identity challenges for, 1, 3, 34, 44–46, 50; identity policing within community of, 44; oppression factors, 32, 61–62, 63, 118; post-slave trauma syndrome for, 29; psychological oppression for, 63, 118; race-neutrality beliefs and, 53; racism for, distinctive nature of, 26–27; slavery, 15, 29, 39–40; stereotypes, 11–12, 26–27, 114–15, 118; white-passing factors and challenges for, 5, 9, 32, 39, 41, 107
alienation, 3–4, 7–8, 16–17, 25, 43–44, 72
Americanization, 7, 9–10, 17, 19–22, 122–23
Anzaldua, Gloria, 8, 16–17, 20
Appiah, Kwame Anthony, 20, 35–36, 45, 46, 47, 116
Argo, 6, 22, 27, 42
Aristotle, 70–72
Arneson, Richard, 86–87
Aronson, Joshua, 15, 116–17

Asian Americans, 27, 28, 31, 34, 40
assimilation, 7, 9–10, 17, 19–22, 122–23

Bartky, Sandra, 13, 15, 63, 72, 117
Beeghly, Erin, 12
Bernstein, Mark, 111
biracial experience, 22–23, 27, 32–33, 44
Blum, Lawrence, 11, 14–15
Brison, Susan, 59
Bush, George W., 12

capabilities: as basis of rights, 91–92, 97, 99, 105; constitutional protections and, 77, 81–82, 86–88, 95–98; definition and types of, 66, 76–78; emotional wellbeing and, 76, 103–5, 112; government role in guaranteeing, 88, 97, 101, 105, 121, 125; harm as violation of, 63, 75, 76, 103–5; human value and dignity relation to, 77–78, 100, 121; negative, 76; overlapping consensus on, 78; personal autonomy and, 79–80; primary goods relation to, 84–85; restoration of undermined, 125, 126, 127; as rights-generating,

74, 75, 88–89, 99–100; self-stereotyping impact on, 13, 121; social aspects of, 76–77, 102–3; threshold level for, 86–87
capabilities approach: autonomy of choice and, 81–85, 99; capabilities outlined in, 76–78; cultural autonomy and, 79–80; to education, 98; employment and, 101; group membership objection to, 87–88; imperialism and objections to, 81–82, 83–84, 98–99; individual treatment and, 79, 87; Iranian American experience and, 85–86, 101–5; objections and corresponding responses to, 79–88, 98–99; as oppression assessment, 66, 73, 74, 75, 100–101, 104, 105, 113; psychological elements and, 76–77, 104–5; to rights, 74, 75, 88–89, 91–92, 94, 95, 96, 97–101, 105, 120–21; rights as claims relation to, 94, 98; rights-based justice approach compared with, 98–101; subjective welfarism contrasted with, 78; threshold objection to, 86–87; universalism objection to, 81–85; utilitarian social justice calculations contrasted with, 78–79; wellbeing approach relation to, 79–81, 95–96, 98, 103–4, 112; women's rights examples and, 82–85, 99
Card, Claudia, 1
Charlesworth, Hilary, 81–82, 84
coercion: defining, 68–70; empirical compared with moral theory of, 60; ignorance role in, 71; justified, 62; noncompliance consequences relation to, 68–69; oppression and, 60, 62–64, 66–72, 73; subordinate/privilege dynamic and, 69, 71–72; voluntary action contrasted with, 66–72
communism, 91

constitutional protections, 77, 81–82, 86–88, 95–98
Cottingham, John, 17–18
credibility, 113
Cudd, Ann, 55, 60–66, 69, 73, 123
cultural essentialism, 45, 46, 48
cultural imperialism, 45, 56, 75, 83–84, 112
culture: as fluid and changing, 46, 82–83; identity based on shared, 24, 45–46, 50; identity policing with adoption of white, 42, 44; marginalized groups identification with, 43–46, 50; preservation and racial emancipation, 45; rejection of, 9; stereotypes informing views of, 43–44

Declaration of Independence, 75
Deutsch, Morton, 111, 112, 125
Donnelly, Jack, 75
Du Bois, W. E. B., 24
Dworkin, Ronald, 91–92

education: capabilities approach to, 98; coercion by lack of choice in, 69–70; entitlement theory and access to, 90–91; oppression fight and, 120, 125, 126
emotional wellbeing. *See* trauma; wellbeing, emotional and physical
employment: capabilities approach and, 101; Iranian Americans stereotypes role in, 37, 109; oppression relation to nature of, 54, 56; race questions with application for, 22, 25, 30, 44; white-passing and diversity quotas in, 25
entitlement theory, 90–92
Espiritu, Yen Le, 31
essentialism. *See* cultural essentialism; racial essentialism
ethnicity: African Americans and, 39–40; appearance factors with, 41,

46–48; cultural factors in defining, 43–46; essentialism dangers with identity and, 48–52; identification with race contrasted with, 43; identity construction and, 39, 40–41, 44; Iranian American experience of, 5, 6, 41–48; labels and, 49; political environment around, 23; race contrasted with, 39–47, 52; racial constructivism and, 39; white-passing identity and choice of, 39, 44
existential creed, 3

Feinberg, Joel, 94, 96
feminist theory, 2–3, 54, 103
films and media, 6–7, 12, 22, 27, 42, 126
Freire, Paulo, 125
Frye, Marilyn, 12, 54, 57, 64–65

gaslighting, 113
genital mutilation, female, 45, 68–69
Gould, Stephen Jay, 48
Greek ethnicity, 5, 22

harms: capabilities violation and, 63, 75, 76, 103–5; of cultural imperialism, 45, 56, 75, 112; economic, 109–10; emotional and physical, intersection, 108; moral exclusion, 111–12; oppression/racism-related, 27, 32, 57, 61, 64, 73, 75, 77, 104, 105, 106–18, 124; of self-hatred and shame, 8–9, 13, 64, 117–18; of self-stereotyping, 9–10, 13, 114–15, 116, 120–21, 126; with sense of injustice, 112–13; stereotyping, 9–10, 12–14, 15, 26, 114–15, 116–17, 120–21, 126; with white-passing, 32, 115–18. *See also* wellbeing, emotional and physical
Harvey, Jean, 55
Haslanger, Sally, 24–25, 26, 29–30, 31–32, 46–47
hate groups/crimes, 38, 109, 111
Hispanic label, 49

Hobbes, Thomas, 97
homeplace, 16–17
hooks, bell, 16–17
Howard, Judith, 11, 13, 114–15

identity and identity development: African Americans challenges with, 1, 3, 34, 44–46, 50; alliances in fight against oppression relation to, 43, 49, 51–52, 121–22; authenticity factors in, 17, 18, 20, 46, 47–48, 50, 116; with biracial experience, 22–23, 27, 32–33, 44; class differences factors in, 50; essentialism dangers with, 48–52; ethnicity role in, 39, 40–41, 44; fluid nature of, 8, 17; fractured, 20; in-between worlds and, 7–10, 16–17; integrity and, 17–20; Iranian Americans approach and challenges with, 8–9, 30–31, 37–38, 42, 44, 50–51; Iranians in exile and crisis of, 41–42; multiple racial maps and, 20; policing within communities, 42, 44; political factors in, 38, 49; psychological and social elements of, 27, 48–49; racialization contrast with self, 47, 48–52; racism impact on, 18–19; shared culture role, 24, 45–46, 50; stereotypes impacting, 3, 14, 38, 114. *See also* white-passing identity
immigration/immigrants: alliances, 121–22; identity development for, 19–20; in-between worlds for, 8, 9–10, 16–17; Iranian Americans motivation for, 42, 102; teenage, 4–5. *See also* Iranian Americans; Mexican Americans
imperialism, 45, 56, 75, 81–84, 98–99, 112
imprisonment, 12, 26, 58, 61, 62, 78
in-between worlds, 7–10, 16–17
Indian Americans (Asian), 40
in-group/out-group dynamic, 41, 42, 46, 48, 49

integrity, 17–20, 76
Iran: culture shifts in, 82–83; diaspora diversity from, 65; diaspora from, identity crisis for, 41–42; emotions oppressed in, 77; gender inequalities in, 51, 60; Iranian American alienation while visiting, 25; Iranian American men approach to women's issues in, 50–51; *Not Without My Daughter* on escape from, 6–7; nuclear threat narrative about, 6; US public opinion in 1980s of, 5; US relations historically with, 4–6, 12; US relations with, Iranian Americans impacted by, 4–5, 8, 37, 65, 108–9; US travel ban on, 5–6
Iran hostage crisis (1979): *Argo* depiction of, 6, 22, 27, 42; Iranian American economic oppression after, 109–10; negative stereotypes arising from, 4, 13, 15–16, 21, 51, 65, 109–10
Iranian Americans: alienation for, 7, 25, 44; capabilities approach relation to, 85–86, 101–5; census category lacking for, 38; cultural oppression experience for, 45; dehumanization of, 109, 126; discrimination experience example, 13–14; economic oppression for, 109–10; ethnicity experience for, 5, 6, 41–48; gender differences in ethnic identity for, 51; hate groups/crimes against, 38, 109; identity approach and challenges for, 8–9, 30–31, 37–38, 42, 44, 50–51; identity crisis for second and third generation, 42; identity policing within community of, 42; immigration motivation for, 42, 102; in-between worlds for, 8, 9–10; Iran hostage crisis impact on stereotyping of, 4, 13, 15–16, 21, 51, 65, 109–10; Iran-Iraq War impact for, 4, 65, 110; laws restricting, 13; marginalization process for, 56; materialism stereotypes of, 6, 12, 15; men, stereotypes of, 6–7, 27, 42, 51, 72; men role in identity for, 50–51; Mexican American struggles kinship to, 121–22; Obama administration and, 5, 23; oppression experiences for, 6–7, 12, 22, 27, 42, 45, 56, 64, 65, 102–5, 108–10, 122–23, 126–27; oppression fight alliances for, 121–22; Persian identity for, 37–38; personal actions reflecting on community of, 7, 15; psychological oppression for, 64; racial essentialism and identity conflicts for, 30–31, 50; racialization experience for, 22, 33, 36–39, 49, 108, 115; racialized as Mexican Americans, 22, 49, 108, 115; racism avoidance methods for, 5, 6, 9, 102–3; racism experiences for, 5–6, 13–14, 102–3, 108–9; socioeconomic status for, 27, 37, 50, 65, 75, 101–2, 110, 122, 123; stereotypes, sources and impacts of, 4, 6–7, 12, 13, 15–16, 21, 27, 37, 42, 51, 65, 72, 102, 109–10, 115, 126; Trump rhetoric and policies on, 5, 18, 27; US-Iran relations impacting experience for, 4–6, 8, 37, 65, 108–9; white culture identification of, 44; white-passing for, 9, 13, 21, 22–23, 27, 115; women, oppression experience for, 102–3; women, stereotypes about, 3
Iranians in Texas (Mobasher), 38
Iran-Iraq War, 4, 65, 110
Irish Americans, 47, 108
Islamic Revolution (1978), 4, 15–16, 41–42, 60

Japanese Americans, 5, 51

Kantian perspectives, 77–78
King, Martin Luther, Jr., 27, 123

LaBossiere, Michael C., 49
language: racialization and, 36, 37; skills barriers, 4, 112, 115
libertarian theories, 89–90, 91
Lipstick Jihad (Moaveni), 25
Locke, John, 97
Lugones, Maria, 16

Mahmoody, Betty, 6–7
Mallon, Ron, 24, 35, 37, 43, 107
Mappes, Thomas, 68, 69
marginalization process, 56, 112, 124
marginalized groups: alliance formation among different, 41, 49, 51–52, 121–22; ancestry and physical appearance identification for, 46–48; common goal for, 42–43; cultural identification of, 43–46, 50; cultural imperialism and, 45, 56, 112; identity policing within, 42, 44; racialization of, 31–32; systemic change obstacles for, 19
Martin, Rex, 74, 75, 92, 93–94
materialism, 6, 12, 15
media and films, 6–7, 12, 22, 27, 42, 126
mental health. *See* psychological elements; wellbeing, emotional and physical
Mexican Americans: alienation experience for, 43; employment application race options for, 22, 30; employment stereotypes and, 54; gender differences in stereotypes of, 51; Iranian Americans in Texas racialized as, 22, 49, 108, 115; Iranian American struggles relation to, 121–22; racial realist views of, 28; stereotypes, 15, 51, 54; white culture identification for, 43–44, 50
Middle Easterners: Asian Indians targeted as, 40; men, stereotypes of, 6–7, 12, 23, 72; racial realist views of, 28. *See also* Iranian Americans
Mills, Charles, 31–32, 33–35

missionism, 82
Moaveni, Azadeh, 25
Mobasher, Mohsen, 5, 38, 41, 109
Montague, Phillip, 92–93
moral exclusion, 111–12
Moses, Michele, 18, 19
Muslims, 10, 23, 31, 42

Native Americans, 28, 29, 40
Nazis, 45, 123
Nelson, Julie A., 103
9/11 terrorist attacks, 5
Not Without My Daughter, 6–7, 22, 27, 42
Nozick, Robert, 62, 89, 92
Nussbaum, Martha: on capabilities approach, 66, 74, 76–78, 83–86, 87, 88–89, 95, 98–101; on cultural imperialism objection, 83–84; on human functioning and dignity protections, 45–46; on primary goods and capabilities, 85; on rights, 88–89, 96, 98–101; on shame and affirming negative stereotypes, 13; on threshold levels for capabilities, 87; on women's rights, 83

Obama administration, 5, 23
objectification, 72
objectively constructed folk theory, 35–38, 40, 47, 52
oppression: for African Americans, 32, 61–62, 63, 118; alliances in fight against, 43, 49, 51–52, 121–22; birdcage analogy and, 12, 57, 64–65; capabilities approach for assessment of, 66, 73, 74, 75, 100–101, 104, 105, 113; categories/faces of, 55–57, 66; coercion factor in, 60, 62–64, 66–72, 73; community building efforts in fight against, 126–27; Cudd criteria for, 55, 60, 61–62, 73; cultural imperialism and, 45, 56, 112; economic, 109–10; education role in fight against, 120, 125, 126;

emotional wellbeing and, 27, 57, 61, 64, 73, 75, 77, 105; employment and, 54, 56; fighting, methods and factors in, 43, 49, 51–52, 119–26; Freire on approach to, 125; gaslighting and, 113; government role in, 119–20, 121; group membership criteria and, 57, 65, 73, 87, 107–8; harms related to, 27, 32, 57, 61, 64, 73, 75, 77, 104, 105, 106–18, 124; humor and jokes role in, 55; injustice relation to, 58–59, 112–13; Iranian Americans experience of, 6–7, 12, 22, 27, 42, 45, 56, 64, 65, 102–5, 108–10, 122–23, 126–27; liberals unknowing perpetuation of, 53–54; listening to others in fight against, 125; mental attitude in fight against, 127; metaphysical background to theories of, 66, 74; moral exclusion with, 111–12; multiple forces together creating, 57, 65; perpetrators of, criteria for, 61–62; powerlessness with, 56, 114; psychological elements of, 13, 14, 27, 60, 63–64, 72–73, 77, 103–5, 116–18; race-neutrality beliefs perpetuating, 53–54; with racialization, 102; resilient autonomy and, 58–60, 66; rights role in fighting, 120–21; sense of injustice harms with, 112–13; social belonging and, 102–3; social mobility barriers and, 54–55; stereotypes relation to, 13, 14, 54, 64, 72–73, 114–15, 116–18, 121–23; stereotypes used in fighting, 121–22; subordinate/privilege dynamic in, 56, 61–62, 72–73, 119; subtle forms and indirect forces of, 55, 71–72; suicide and, 27, 77; systematicity criterion of, 57, 59, 64–65, 73; theories of, 53–66, 73, 74, 108; theory amended from Cudd, 62–66, 73; trauma and, 103; unified theory of, debates on, 55, 56, 57, 58; unknowing perpetuation of, 53–54, 61, 119; victim blaming and, 61–62, 123; violence with, 56, 59, 108–9; voluntary action and, 63–64, 67–72, 73, 85, 114–16, 127; white-passing and harms of, 32, 115–18; Young theory of, 53, 55–57, 66, 108; Zutlevics theory of, 55, 58–60, 73
oppression/advantage test, 32
Ortega, Mariana, 1, 8, 20

Peffer, Rodney, 94
Persian identity, 5, 12, 37–38, 110, 115
pessimism, 127
phenomenology, 1–3
Phillips, Anne, 85
physical wellbeing. *See* violence; wellbeing, emotional and physical
Piper, Adrian, 9, 32, 41, 116
poverty, 1, 19, 78–79, 87, 101, 111
powerlessness, 56, 114
primary goods, 84–85
privilege. *See* subordinate/privilege dynamic
psychological elements: capabilities approach and, 76–77, 104–5; of identity development, 27, 48–49; oppression and, 13, 14, 27, 60, 63–64, 72–73, 77, 103–5, 116–18
Puddifoot, Katherine, 10

race: ancestry and physical appearance factors with, 46–48; authenticity debates on identification with, 47–48, 50, 116; categories, criteria for determining, 33–34; categories for biracial individuals, 32–33; categories of, 23, 24, 28–34; conceptions about, guiding factors in, 26; conceptual, descriptive, and analytical approach to studying, 24–25; cultural experience in defining, 24, 34–36, 39, 43–46; employment application questions on, 22, 25, 30, 44; ethnicity contrasted with, 39–47, 52; experiential account of, 34–35; fluidity and changing nature of, 24, 31, 35–36, 43, 51; folk theory of, 35, 37, 107; as given not inherent, 25, 29, 39; Haslanger defining, 25, 29–30, 31–32, 46–47; identification with ethnicity contrasted with, 43; Iranian American experience of ethnicity and, 41–48; metaphysical realities and defining, 29–30, 46, 47; neutrality perpetuating oppression, 53–54; "not-traveling constraint" in categorizing, 24, 26, 35–36, 52, 108; objective approaches to, 28, 29, 35–36; objectively constructed folk theory of, 35–38, 40, 47, 52; political division and factors around, 23, 38, 51, 116; as social construction, 25, 29–30, 46–47; stereotypes forming concepts of, 26–27; subjective approaches to, 33–34; theories of, 1, 23, 24–25, 31–36, 120; vague criterial theory of, 35–36; white-passing and definition of, 31–32, 39. *See also* ethnicity

race theory, 1, 23, 24–25, 120

racial constructivism: essentialism contrasted with, 24, 30; ethnicity choice and, 39; "not-traveling constraint" of race view under, 35, 36; as objective approach to race, 28; objectively constructed folk theory and, 35–38, 40, 47, 52; racial realist views contrasted with, 29–30

racial essentialism (racialism): authenticity of identity and, 50; cultural essentialism relation to, 45; debate on, 26; identity development and dangers of, 48–52; in-group/out-group dichotomy creation with, 41, 42, 46, 48; Iranian Americans viewed under, 30–31, 50; ontological consensus undermining, 24; racial constructivism in contrast to, 24, 30; racialization and racism fueled by, 24; racial realism relation to, 28; stereotyping and, 26

racialization: Asian American, 27, 28, 31, 34, 40; biracial experience of, 22–23, 27, 32–33, 44; class differences and, 50; criteria, 107; defining, 23; difference across time and place, 24, 31, 108; folk theory on, 35, 37, 107; group membership and, 107–8; hate groups/crime and, 38; Iranian Americans experience with, 22, 33, 36–39, 49, 108, 115; of Irish Americans, 47, 108; language and, 36, 37; of minority groups, 31–32; objectively constructed folk theory on, 35–38, 40, 47, 52; oppression with, 102; racial essentialism justification for, 24; self-identity contrasted with, 47, 48–52; subordinate/privilege dynamic in, 31–32, 35, 37, 38, 107; voluntary action and, 107–8; wellbeing impacted by, 24, 25, 107, 108, 116; white-passing and, 31–32, 39, 44, 107, 115–16

racial realism, 28, 29–30

racism: African American, distinctive nature of, 26–27; children learning, 27; communities impacted differently by, 27; cultural imperialism and, 45, 56, 112; economic harms of, 109–10; emotional and physical wellbeing impacts from, 104, 106–7; fight against, methods and factors in, 119–26; generational differences in experiences of, 28–29; harms related with, 27, 32, 57, 61, 64, 73, 75, 77, 104, 105, 106–18, 124; identity development impacted by, 18–19; inferiority claims behind, 23, 30; Iranian Americans experience of, 5–6, 13–14, 102–3, 108–10; Iranian Americans methods of avoiding, 5, 6, 9, 102–3; moral exclusion with,

111–12; performance in society relation to, 30; racial essentialism and, 24; sense of injustice harms with, 112–13; Sikhs confused with Muslims and, 23, 31; socioeconomic success relation to, 102; Trump rhetoric and policy of, 3, 5, 18, 23, 27; violence with, 56, 59, 108–9. *See also* oppression

rape, 59, 76

Rawls, John, 84–85

research approach and inspiration, 1–3, 22–23, 52

resilient autonomy, 58–60, 66

Reynolds, Kathrine, 114, 121–22

rights: capabilities approach to, 74, 75, 88–89, 91–92, 94, 95, 96, 97–101, 105, 120–21; capabilities as basis of, 91–92, 97, 99, 105; capabilities role in generation of, 74, 75, 88–89, 99–100; civil, 96–97, 98, 100, 109, 110; as claims, 75, 92–94, 96, 98; consequentialist understanding of, 94–95; constitutional protections and, 77, 81–82, 86–88, 95–98; culpability question and, 93–94; Declaration of Independence on, 75; duty and, 93–94; as entitlements, 75, 89–92, 96; government role in protecting, 96–97, 98, 101, 105, 121; justice approach with capabilities compared to, 98–101; justifying, 96–97; libertarian theories of, 89–90, 91; lying and, as claims, 92–93; moral grounding for, 88; natural, 96, 97, 99–100, 105; negative, 90–92, 120; Nussbaum on, 88–89, 96, 98–101; positive, 90–92, 96, 100, 120; Sen on political, 89; situational, 74; social contract theory of, 94–95; theories of, 74–75, 89–90, 91, 94–97, 105; welfare, objections to, 90; wellbeing, 75, 94–96, 98, 121; as western concept, 82, 98–99, 101; women's, 45, 50–51, 68–69, 82–85, 99

Root, Michael, 35, 36

Schindler, Oskar, 123

self-hatred and shame, 8–9, 13, 64, 117–18

self-knowledge and evaluation, 10, 18, 33, 124

self-stereotyping, 9–10, 13, 114–15, 116, 120–21, 126

Seligman, Martin, 127

Sen, Amartya, 66, 74, 76–78, 85, 89

sexual violence, 51, 59, 76

The Shahs of Sunset, 6–7, 12, 22, 27, 42

shame and self-hatred, 8–9, 13, 64, 117–18

Shelby, Tommie, 26–27, 39, 45, 49–50

Sikhs, 23, 31

slavery, 15, 29, 39–40

Smith, Tara, 90–91, 92, 96

social learning theory, 29

social mobility, 54–55

standpoint theory, 2–3

Steele, Claude, 14, 15, 116–17

stereotypes/stereotyping: African American discrimination and, 11–12, 26–27, 114–15, 118; anxiety with navigating, 15, 17; Asian Americans, 27; assimilation relation to, 9–10, 21; bi-directional nature of, 123; birdcage analogy in impacts of, 12; cognitive distortions with, 11, 14; cultural views informed by, 43–44; defining, 10–11; existential credo relation to, 3; films and media perpetuating negative Iranian, 6–7, 27, 42, 51, 72, 126; gaslighting and, 113; gender differences in, 51; generalization contrasted with, 10; harms of, 9–10, 12–14, 15, 26, 114–15, 116–17, 120–21, 126; identity development impacted by, 3, 14, 38,

114; imprisonment relation to, 3–4, 12; in-between worlds and, 9–10, 16–17; internalization of negative, 13, 15, 30, 33, 63, 68, 72–73, 86, 106, 114, 116, 118; of Iranian Americans, sources and impacts of, 4, 6–7, 12, 13, 15–16, 21, 27, 37, 42, 51, 65, 72, 102, 109–10, 115, 126; learning, 11; Mexican American, 15, 51, 54; moral distortions with, 11, 14; Muslim, 10, 23, 31; oppression fight and uniting along, 121–22; oppression relation to negative, 13, 14, 54, 64, 72–73, 114–15, 116–18, 121–23; overcoming, 10; performance anxiety from, 15; pluralist view of, 12; pressures for adhering to or contradicting, 15, 27, 51; psychological oppression with, 13, 14, 72–73; race concepts informed by, 26–27; racial designation shift with, 43; racial essentialism and, 26; racial realists and, 28; research on, 20–21; self, 9–10, 13, 114–15, 116, 120–21, 126; shame and self-hatred with, 8–9, 13, 117; threat, 14–16, 116–17; victim blaming and, 11, 13, 115; wellbeing impacts from, 12, 13, 15, 26, 30, 33, 63, 68, 72–73, 86, 106, 114, 116–17, 118; white-passing and, 21, 33
subordinate/privilege dynamic: coercion and, 69, 71–72; cultural imperialism and, 56, 112; folk theory of race and, 37, 107; oppression relation to, 56, 61–62, 72–73, 119; racialization and, 31–32, 35, 37, 38, 107; victim-blaming and, 123; white-passing and, 32
suicide, 27, 77

Texas, 22, 38, 49, 108, 115
trauma: generational, inheritance of, 29, 30; of 9/11 and aftermath, 5; oppression and, 103; post-slave, for African Americans, 29; racialized, 4, 28–29, 30; self-integrity and, 18
Trump, Donald, 3, 5, 10, 18, 23, 27, 78

US-Iran relations, 4–6, 8, 12, 37, 65, 108–9

Vallentyne, Peter, 79–81
Van Dyke, Sandra, 120
victim-blaming, 11, 13, 61–62, 115, 123
violence: moral exclusion and, 111–12; with racism/oppression, 56, 59, 108–9; sexual, 51, 59, 76
voluntary action: Aristotle on, 70–72; coercion contrasted with, 66–72; oppression and, 63–64, 67–72, 73, 85, 114–16, 127; racialization and, 107–8

wellbeing, emotional and physical: capabilities and, 76, 103–5, 112; capabilities approach relation to, 79–81, 95–96, 98, 103–4, 112; government role in protecting, 103; group membership and, 42; Iranian Americans experience around, 5, 27, 65, 102–3; moral exclusion and, 111–12; oppression relation to, 27, 57, 61, 64, 73, 75, 77, 105; physical and emotional harms intersection in, 108; racialization impact on, 24, 25, 107, 108, 116; for racial minorities compared with white community, 103–4; racism impacts on, 104, 106–7; rights around, 75, 94–96, 98, 121; stereotypes impacting, 12, 13, 15, 26, 30, 33, 63, 68, 72–73, 86, 106, 114, 116–17, 118; white-passing and, 115–18. *See also* psychological elements; trauma
white-passing identity: for African Americans, 5, 9, 32, 39, 41, 107; authenticity and race debate with, 47–48, 116; critics of, 116; employment discrimination and,

25; ethnic identity choice relation to, 39, 44; family and friend relationships impacted by, 9; for Iranian Americans, 9, 13, 21, 22–23, 27, 115; for Mexican Americans and, 43–44; oppression/advantage test and, 32; oppression harms with, 32, 115–18; race definition and, 31–32, 39; racialization factors with, 31–32, 39, 44, 107, 115–16; racialized trauma and, 28–29; shame and, 9, 117; social capital with, 19; stereotypes and, 21, 33; subordinate/privilege dynamic and, 32

Williams, Patricia, 53
women's rights, 45, 50–51, 68–69, 82–85, 99

Yancy, George, 1, 3
Young, Iris Marion, 53, 55–57, 66, 108

Zack, Naomi, 1, 29
Zutlevics, T. L., 55, 58–60, 73

About the Author

Roksana Alavi is an associate (term) professor of interdisciplinary studies at the University of Oklahoma College of Professional and Continuing Studies, as well as an affiliate faculty member in the Iranian studies, and women and gender studies programs. Before teaching for the university, Dr. Alavi was an assistant professor of philosophy in South Texas College.

Alavi received her Ph.D. in philosophy from the University of Kansas as well as a graduate certificate in women's studies. Her research focuses on identity formation, race, rights, stereotyping and oppression in the field of social and political philosophy. She has recently focused on teaching and on researching the issues of human trafficking, race, and ethical leadership.